GRANDPARENTS
Michigan Style

Places to Go & Wisdom to Share

by Mike Link and Kate Crowley

Adventure Publications
Cambridge, Minnesota

DEDICATION:

To Matthew, Aren, Ryan, Annalise, and Teagan, who have taught us the magic of grandparenting.

PHOTO CREDITS:

Front cover: Middle inset by Mike Link and Kate Crowley; all other photos via Shutterstock

Back cover: All images by Mike Link and Kate Crowley

All photos are copyright Mike Link and Kate Crowley unless otherwise noted.

SS Badger photo courtesy of Lake Michigan Carferry.

Colonial Michilimackinac and Historic Mill Creek Discovery Park photos courtesy of Mackinac State Historic Parks.

Page 26 and *Bonding & Bridging* images via Shutterstock.

Cover and book design by Jonathan Norberg

10 9 8 7 6 5 4 3 2 1

First Edition 2009
Second edition 2017
Copyright 2017 by Mike Link and Kate Crowley
Published by Adventure Publications
An imprint of AdventureKEEN
820 Cleveland Street South
Cambridge, Minnesota 55008
(800) 678-7006
www.adventurepublications.net
All rights reserved
Printed in U.S.A.
ISBN: 978-1-59193-730-2

Table of Contents

Introduction 6

A Word from Mike Link 8

A Word from Kate Crowley. 10

How to Use This Book 11

Location Map 12

Charles H. Wright Museum of African American History 14

Michigan Science Center. 16

Detroit Zoo. 18

Greenfield Village 20

Henry Ford Museum. 22

Ford Rouge Factory Tour. 24

Dossin Great Lakes Museum 26

Abbott Magic Company 28

Air Zoo 30

Kalamazoo Nature Center 32

Holland Tulips. 34

Butterfly Gardens. 36

Lena Meijer Children's Garden at Frederik Meijer
Gardens & Sculpture Park. 38

Michigan History Museum 40

Michigan State Capitol 42

Festival Fun in Frankenmuth. 44

Marshall M. Fredericks Sculpture Garden & Museum. 46

Hartwick Pines State Park and Logging Museum. 48

Interlochen Center for the Arts 50

Tall Ship Sailing. 52

Sleeping Bear Dunes National Lakeshore. 54

Oden State Fish Hatchery 56

Mackinac Island. 58

Historic Mill Creek Discovery Park 60

Colonial Michilimackinac 62

Museum of Ojibwa Culture 64

The Locks at Sault Ste. Marie 66

The Birds of Whitefish Point 68

Tahquamenon Falls State Park 70

Great Lakes Shipwreck Museum 72

Seney National Wildlife Refuge 74

Fayette Historic State Park 76

Pictured Rocks National Lakeshore 78

Marquette Maritime Museum 80

Michigan Iron Industry Museum 82

U.S. Ski and Snowboard Hall of Fame and Museum 84

Sylvania Wilderness 86

Porcupine Mountains Wilderness State Park 88

Keweenaw National Historical Park 90

Fort Wilkins Historic State Park 92

Isle Royale National Park 94

Amtrak 96

Art Museums 98

Beaches 100

Biking 102

Botanical Gardens 104

Campfire 106

Canoeing 108

Cemetery Visit 110

Children's Museums 112

Cooking Together 114

Drive-In Restaurants 116

Ethnic Celebrations 118

Farmers Markets 120

Farm Life 122

Ferry across Lake Michigan 124

Fireworks 126

Fishing 128

Grandparents Day 130

Kirtland's Warblers 132

Kite Flying 134

Libraries 136

Lighthouses 138

Michigan Weather 140

Petoskey Stones 142

Picking Cherries 144

Picnicking 146

Pow Wows 148

Urban Parks 150

Waterfalls 152

Winter Festivals 154

Index 156

About the Authors 160

Introduction

Grandparents Michigan Style is for today's grandparents who want to spend more time discovering the world with their grandchildren. This book is about opportunities for adults and children to have fun, laugh, and share. Of course, Michigan is ripe with more possibilities than we can cover, but this is a place to get started. We decided to write this book because of our experiences with our grandchildren—three boys and two girls. They provide us with a lot of fun, but we also have a responsibility to them. We can use our time together to help them learn and grow as individuals.

In writing this book we've had to stop and think about the knowledge we gained, how we learned valuable life lessons, and how we could pass our wisdom to our grandchildren. With the changing times, we found that several experiences have become endangered—solitude, silence, open space, dark night skies, free time, reading books, and home-cooked food.

CONSIDER THE FOLLOWING CHANGES:

1. Farms are no longer a part of most children's experiences. In 1900, farmers accounted for 40 percent of our census. By 1990, the total fell below 2 percent.

2. Open space was once a playground. Now, it is slated for development. Children are left with only fenced yards and indoor locations.

3. The "out in the country" experience is disappearing. Urban sprawl means an hour's drive from the inner city to any country areas.

4. Tree climbing is more difficult now. There are few open areas of trees for Jacks and Jills to climb magic beanstalks.

5. The chance to be bored—which is an opportunity to be creative—isn't often in the schedule. Children are signed up for every organized activity and training available, eliminating family time and free time.

6. Sports used to be for fun. Now some parents have children choose a sport, and then send them to summer camps where winning is what matters.

7. Canning, pickling and baking—all of those wonderful activities that filled the root cellars and pantries of the past—are less common.

Today's world has seen some bad and dangerous trends. Fast food (and obesity) is the norm. Meth and other deadly drugs flood our cities, our neighborhoods, and our schools.

Fortunately, our grandchildren have us. The role of the grandparent can be different than it was when we were kids, and we can adapt, too. Grandparents have many opportunities:

1. Grandparents are living longer than ever before and can influence their grandchildren longer.

2. Parents work long days, filled with busy hours.

3. Grandparents can provide children with quiet times, new experiences, and more play.

4. Grandparents can help introduce children to healthy food; we have the time to prepare it and present it.

5. Children may gain from perspectives other than those of their peers, and they may benefit from our guidance and insight.

We may be able to involve the extended family in more activities and be part of the new modern family of the twenty-first century.

That's not to say we should take on the role of mother and father. Instead, our place is to supplement a child's parents, to help them wherever our help is wanted and needed. Let's use the time we have with our grandchildren to instill in them important values, to teach them about the world around them, and to help shape them into better people.

A Word from Mike Link

In 2010, Kate and I walked around Lake Superior and enjoyed two months on the shore, cobbles, beaches, rocks, and trails. Our Full Circle Superior Adventure was an exciting personal trek that was the result of my retirement after 38½ years as director of the Audubon Center of the North Woods. It happened because Kate suggested that I symbolically walk away from the Audubon Center to start a new page in my life—and because of our grandkids!

It might seem strange to think that our grandchildren would cause us to walk 1,555 miles in 145 days, but I will share our philosophy of what it means to be grandparents (and no, we were not walking away from them). Our five grandchildren—Matthew, Aren, Ryan, Annalise, and Teagan—have brought great love and joy to our lives. Each time we spend time with them and watch them experience something new, we also see the world anew. We believe that they, and all grandchildren, have the right to live in a world every bit as beautiful as we have known.

As we spent time with our grandchildren, taking them outside, helping them discover birds and butterflies, playing in the water, floating sticks, and skipping rocks, we considered what we could give them—what would be their inheritance? While we are alive, we will give them attention and companionship, which we consider the best gifts. Like all grandparents, we still give them toys and books, but as much as possible we want to give them the gift of our time through shared travel, experiences, and lifelong memories.

When we became grandparents and started this series of books, we asked friends how many remembered gifts their grandparents had given them. We watched these adults struggle to think of a toy, game, or outfit that they associated with their grandparents. Some could remember one or two things, but inevitably they remembered activities they did with their grandparents, and not the things they were given.

Growing up, my grandparents were essential to my life. My father, Howard Link, came home from World War II with a disease contracted in New Guinea, one the Army thought might kill him. They sent him to a military hospital in Washington, and my mom, Alta (Prock) Link, took a train across the country to see him and marry him. For my mom, that was the one big expedition of her life and one that seems out of character. But love motivated her.

I was born nearly two years later in December 1945, and I entered a strange world. My dad was unable to get a steady job because of the lingering effects of the disease, and this created a difficult childhood with too much drink, too little money, and a new home in a new small town every few months. But my mom and dad were strong and determined people. Eventually, my dad got a job with Honeywell, and he stayed with it until he retired. My mom was the homemaker, my loving companion, and always smiling and worried about everyone else.

My dad's job was second shift, 3 p.m. to midnight, and often he would work an additional two hours to bring in more money. He gave up both smoking and drinking—cold turkey. My life was pleasant, but for me, he was often absent—sleeping through breakfast and working when I returned home. We lived in poor neighborhoods and still continued to move, but now every few years instead of months. He continued to work to make our lives better, taking a second job on weekends as a mechanic.

His relationship with his mom and dad was outstanding, and that was wonderful for me because Bert Link and Stella (Kahl) Link accepted me into their home and opened up my life. Grandpa drove a laundry truck; Grandma sold fabric for Herberger's. Their home in Rice Lake, Wisconsin, was a safe and loving sanctuary. Grandpa took the place of my dad in many ways because he taught me to throw a ball, took me along on his laundry route, taught me to drive, and set an example that was always positive. Grandma took me blackberry picking and made the greatest blackberry pies and coffee cakes in the world. Only her sugar cookies could measure up to them. Like my friends, I cannot think of a gift that they gave me, but to this day I am a sucker for anything with blackberry, and I have created a candy dish in my office for my grandkids because Grandpa always had a box of Fanny Farmer chocolates in his desk. My inheritance from them is one of memories, happiness, security, and a home.

So back to the question of what we would leave for our grandchildren—our legacy. We chose fresh water as one theme for our hike because we want to leave the best world for our grandchildren. Fresh air, fresh water, and a healthy planet are things grandparents should leave for future generations. We believe that by taking action ourselves, we set an example for our grandchildren.

Second, we wanted to inspire others to reflect on their legacy. Beyond the material things we leave behind, what will our lives say to future generations? My career has been in education, except for a five-year bump where I was a tax accountant. Eventually, I ended up at the Audubon Center in Sandstone, Minnesota, a residential education center that directly impacted the lives of over 500,000 people and 100 schools during my tenure. We built upon the premise that we are all part of the natural world, and we need to respect the creatures that lived here before us. We wanted everyone to interact with the natural world, discover the beauty of the planet, and make their own commitment to it.

Each place and activity we have included in this book is an opportunity to play, teach, encourage, and share with grandchildren. Each location has a different set of choices for you. We encourage you to relax, remember that the grandchildren are the focus of each visit, and to share—time, love, and smiles.

A Word from Kate Crowley

Most of us, if we're lucky, have known our grandparents. We are even luckier if those grandparents lived nearby and enriched our lives. Until the last 50 years, elders have been integral and respected members of our communities. They transported the stories, the history of the people. They were revered, and children spent time in their company. The Industrial Revolution, while it has brought us lives of relative ease and abundance, has also brought about the gradual decline of the close-knit, extended family.

Much of the knowledge that the elders, the grandparents, carried was tied to life on the land. Older grandparents, and those of the generation who are just now becoming grandparents, are the last generation of which a majority can remember a time when grandparents lived on farms or in small towns. We can recall the easy, simple times spent with these adults who indulged us; we can share memories with a generation being born into a century with untold opportunities and, unfortunately, too many uncertainties.

By the time I was born, I only had two living grandmothers. One lived in California, and I have very fuzzy memories of her. My other grandmother lived just a block away from our house and though her Germanic heritage didn't incline her toward a warm, cuddly exterior, I had over 20 years of close acquaintance with her. I even lived with her for four years during and after high school. She was a working woman into her 80s—ironing clothes for people and caring for one or two elderly people in her home, so she didn't have the time or personality to get down on the floor and play with us. But her house was always open to us, and we wore a path through our neighbors' backyards to get there. She had a few old toys and books for us to play with, and a big old piano, but mostly we came to visit and if we were lucky, on a hot summer day, she'd make us a root beer float.

A Sunday ritual for the first 16 years of my life was dinner at "Ma's," as we called her: roasted chicken, mashed potatoes and gravy, cooked corn, cabbage salad, and either apple or custard pie. I only have to think about it and I'm coming through her front door into a room moist with the steam of cooked vegetables.

Our most firmly held memories of time spent with our grandparents are tied to our senses. These are the things that will stay with children as they grow to adulthood and recall their times spent with their grandparents. That, and laughter.

One of the most mouthwatering memories I have is a summer day picking tomatoes with my grandmother. It was a hot day, and the sun was beating down on us as we moved through the pungent rows of tomato plants. I must have been old enough to be considered trustworthy—she expected me to pick the right ones and handle them properly. What do I remember most about that day? That she packed cheese sandwiches (probably Velveeta) and that I have never eaten anything more delicious than a rich, sweet tomato right off the vine, still holding the sun's heat, with juice running down my chin, followed up by a bite of soft cheese on white bread. The smells and tastes flowed together and I can still see us, joined together by the simple act of harvesting our food.

I have waited a very long time to become a grandmother— and not just because our daughters chose to wait until their 30s to have children. Even when my two children were still pre-teens, I was contemplating grandparent-hood. I packed away all the Fisher-Price toys in their original boxes to share with the next generation and saved as many of their books as possible. I enjoyed raising my two children and I knew I wanted to have similar experiences again, but without the worries and day-to-day concerns that accompany young parenthood. I knew, even then, that as a grandparent I would be able to have fun, play with the kids, act silly, share what I've learned in life with them, but have the luxury of going home at the end of the day to a quiet, clean house.

Now we have three grandsons—all arrived in the span of one year, and two granddaughters to counterbalance all that testosterone, and we are looking forward to years of adventures together. Matthew, Ryan, Aren, Annalise, and Teagan are more precious to me than I could've imagined, just as I know your grandchildren are for you. We are not reliving our childhood through them, as some might think; we are participating in their journey into the future—a future we can only imagine. And we want our journey together to be as much fun and full of learning and discovery as possible. This is why we have written this book—this "field guide"—to help other grandparents find those unique and unforgettable places that will combine fun and facts, history and humor, excitement and enduring memories for you and the special children in your lives.

How to Use This Book

The suggestions in this book are just suggestions. Some experiences are unmatchable anywhere else in the state. Others can be replicated. If you are not near the museum, park, or site we highlight, find a similar place near you. Read our suggestions and pay special attention to "Bonding & Bridging" to tie your visit to a life lesson.

We do not advocate that you become the "wallet" or the "chauffeur." Consider an active participation in friendship and sharing that is enriched by love. We want you to receive the respect due an elder, to share your experience, and to enjoy the love that can flow between generations.

One of the themes of this book is that things change. This is true for every-thing, including the state's attractions. They sometimes close, renovate, or move. When in doubt, *CALL BEFORE YOU LEAVE HOME.*

Location Map

The sites appear in the book in the order below, beginning with those in Detroit and the southeastern part of the state and proceeding toward the northwest.

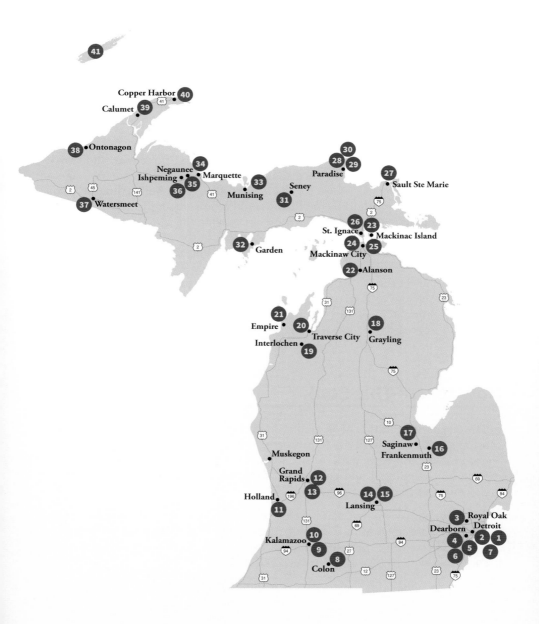

1 Charles H. Wright Museum of African American History 14

2 Michigan Science Center 16

3 Detroit Zoo 18

4 Greenfield Village 20

5 Henry Ford Museum 22

6 Ford Rouge Factory Tour 24

7 Dossin Great Lakes Museum 26

8 Abbott Magic Company 28

9 Air Zoo 30

10 Kalamazoo Nature Center 32

11 Holland Tulips 34

12 Butterfly Gardens 36

13 Lena Meijer Children's Garden . . 38

14 Michigan History Museum 40

15 Michigan State Capitol 42

16 Festival Fun in Frankenmuth 44

17 Marshall M. Fredericks Sculpture Garden & Museum . . . 46

18 Hartwick Pines State Park and Logging Museum 48

19 Interlochen Center for the Arts . . 50

20 Tall Ship Sailing 52

21 Sleeping Bear Dunes National Lakeshore 54

22 Oden State Fish Hatchery 56

23 Mackinac Island 58

24 Historic Mill Creek Discovery Park 60

25 Colonial Michilimackinac 62

26 Museum of Ojibwa Culture 64

27 Locks at Sault Ste. Marie 66

28 The Birds of Whitefish Point 68

29 Tahquamenon Falls State Park 70

30 Great Lakes Shipwreck Museum 72

31 Seney National Wildlife Refuge 74

32 Fayette Historic State Park 76

33 Pictured Rocks National Lakeshore 78

34 Marquette Maritime Museum . . . 80

35 Michigan Iron Industry Museum 82

36 U.S. Ski and Snowboard Hall of Fame and Museum 84

37 Sylvania Wilderness 86

38 Porcupine Mountains Wilderness State Park 88

39 Keweenaw National Historical Park 90

40 Fort Wilkins Historic State Park 92

41 Isle Royale National Park 94

Statewide activities start on page 96

13

Charles H. Wright Museum of African American History

It is appropriate that the world's largest museum dedicated to the African-American experience is located in Detroit, a city where 83 percent of the population is African-American. The museum is a beautiful alabaster stone structure that opened in 1965. It is named for a physician who, along with 30 other civic-minded citizens, sought to create a building and exhibits to honor a people who have risen from the most inhumane conditions this country has ever seen.

But it is not just a monument to that shameful period in our country's history; it is a monument to perseverance, strength, faith, and community. Upon entering the museum, you find yourself in a large, airy rotunda with a glass dome 100 feet in diameter—two feet wider than the Michigan State Capitol dome. The center of the floor is a work of terrazzo art called "Genealogy" and around the edges are the names of prominent African-Americans in history. New names are added each year.

"And Still We Rise" is the flagship exhibit. We recommend that you bring grandchildren old enough to know something about slavery. Start by watching the 15-minute film that begins in Africa, the "Birthplace of Humanity." Then begin a walk through time. Many of the exhibits are scenes with life-size models, background voices, and other sounds that lend an overwhelming sense of reality—you travel from a village in Benin, Africa, to the dark and frightening hold of a slave ship, to the cabin of a slave family, and on through the Civil War and Emancipation, migration to the north and work in the factories, and the Civil Rights Movement. The exhibit ends in a room called "Detroit Rising," with video clips of young people explaining their goals and dreams.

Children too young for this exhibit can visit another called "A is for Africa," with an alphabet mounted along the walls of a circular hallway. Each letter tells something about Africa. Some of the letters have recorded music or voices and some have objects to manipulate; all provide information about animals, places, foods, and people. No matter which exhibit you prefer, this is a place with a strong, hopeful message for everyone who visits.

Bonding & Bridging

Not all the things we do together with our grandchildren need to be about lighthearted amusement. Visits to a museum such as this one let us teach the children about injustices, as well as justice. These exhibits can open up discussion between the generations. As grandparents, you have lived through the Civil Rights Movement. You were alive when schools were integrated in the South and saw all the strife and struggle that involved. You can share with your grandchildren how it felt at that time, regardless of where you lived. Change is always difficult and people sometimes pay great prices for speaking up, but our country has a history of courageous people who questioned slavery or the treatment of American Indians, or who protested wars or the destruction of the environment. Your grandchildren have the potential to make a difference. They live in a world that is much more open to diversity and they need to know that we celebrate all races of people, each of which has contributed to the success of the United States. You can also talk to them about your ancestors—how and when they came to the U.S., and how they struggled to survive.

A WORD TO THE WISE:

Two special events during the year are especially family-oriented and worth involving your grandchildren. In August, there is the African World Festival. For over 35 years this event has combined food, music, poetry, arts, crafts, drumming, and dancing! The second event is Noel Night. In its fourth decade, this is another opportunity for the entire family to enjoy music, food, and storytelling, as well as the fun of making your own ornaments.

AGE OF GRANDCHILD: 9 to teenager

BEST SEASON: All

CONTACT: 315 E Warren Ave., Detroit, MI 48201; (313) 494-5800; www.thewright.org; Noel Night (midtowndetroitinc.org/events); African World Festival (thewright.org/african-world-festival)

ALSO CHECK OUT:

Michigan Freedom Trail (Underground Railroad): www.michigan.gov/freedomtrail

Michigan History Museum: www.michigan.gov/museum

How beautifully the leaves grow old.
How full of light and color are their last days. John Burroughs

Michigan Science Center

In the 1950s and '60s, the word "scientist" was often synonymous with a wild-haired, absent-minded, obsessed man in a lab coat. Today, our image of a scientist is something different altogether: an adventurous biologist roaming the rainforests and jungles, or a highly trained technician banging away at the keyboard while researching superstrings and listening to the background noise of the big bang. Science is no longer just a white coat and a test tube. Science, technology, engineering, and math (STEM) have helped us discover wonders that used to be confined to the world of wizards and magicians. So journey to the Michigan Science Center (MiSci) and help your grandchildren discover science.

With five theaters and live stage shows, it's easy to bring STEM to life at MiSci. Watch live demos on the Chrysler Science Stage, discover electricity in the DTE Energy Sparks Theater, tour the stars in the Dassault Systèmes

Planetarium, and watch a film on the state's largest dome screen in the Chrysler IMAX Dome Theatre.

Visit Spark!Lab to engage in the process of invention with hands-on activities and self-led exploration. Don't miss a variety of special exhibits in the traveling exhibits hall.

But if a show, a lab, and laughs are not enough, there are interactive exhibits. Explore motion with pendulums, flywheels, and hand cranks. Become a modern-day Henry Ford and see how engines work. Refract light, make sounds with a laser beam, and use your own voice for sound experiments. Walk across a miniature Mackinac Bridge or join the production line in the United States Steel Fun Factory. Check out your health in a fun and interactive set of exhibits that focus on the most important laboratory you will ever discover—your body.

Check out the grandparent membership at only $65! You and your grandkids will receive free general admission for a year, discounts, exclusive invitations, access to hundreds of science centers around the world and more.

Bonding & Bridging

Learning sometimes has a negative connotation in our culture, but if we engage our grandchildren in an activity that inspires them, they learn in spite of themselves. The trick is to let things happen naturally. Grandparents have a special way of becoming mentors for children, and by sharing our experience and wisdom, we help children succeed.

Sometimes we bond by teaching children subtle skills, like pacing. When you visit an attraction, like a museum, decide in advance how much time you will spend there, which exhibits you'll see. Let them know that you need to sit down periodically. Take a food break. Sit and talk about what you have seen. Make it clear that you don't want to try to see everything or read everything. Instead, say that you will come back for another visit—and do so. Above all, don't fall into the trap of trying to do too much!

A WORD TO THE WISE:

As much as these wonderful exhibits and presentations can engage the children, you probably will need some time to sit and catch your breath. The children probably will not need or understand the need for a break, so you can divert their attention with one of two excellent options. The first option is the IMAX theater, which is popular and well-known. The Dassault Systèmes Planetarium is the other option. With a three-story dome, marvelous computer-generated effects, music, and narration, this is a trip to space unlike any other. With 40 cameras for special effects, you will be blasted into space as a part of the universe, not just as a passive observer.

AGE OF GRANDCHILD: All

BEST SEASON: Winter, and all the days when the outdoors are less inviting.

CONTACT: Michigan Science Center, 5020 John R St., Detroit, MI 48202; (313) 577-8400; www.mi-sci.org

ALSO CHECK OUT:

Ann Arbor Hands-On Museum: www.aahom.org

Cranbrook Institute of Science: science.cranbrook.edu

Just when I thought I was too old to fall in love again, I became a Grandparent. UNKNOWN

Detroit Zoo

In 1907, a German animal dealer and zoo owner named Carl Hagenbeck revolutionized the zoo world when he developed a new method of exhibiting animals using a moat, rather than bars on cages. The Detroit Zoo opened in 1928 and was designed by a German architect who employed the same approach. In the 89 years since, the Detroit Zoo has continued to improve its exhibits to better serve the animals and the public.

This zoo also incorporates art in a very holistic and beautiful way. It is one of the few zoos in the world to have a permanent art collection. Throughout the zoo you will see sculptures of animals. A good place to begin your visit is the Wildlife Interpretative Gallery, formerly the Bird House. Before you enter the front doors, look up and you will see a beautiful blue tile mosaic of a peacock. This building includes a small theater where a 15-minute film shows the history of the zoo. In another room on the upper level, works of art are

on display. Take a moment to look at these to get the grandchildren thinking about the connection between art and nature, and how many artists use nature for their inspiration. Then head into the Butterfly Garden—a verdant conservatory filled with winged beauties. As you leave this room, you enter an aviary, with more birds, lush vegetation, and the sound of trickling water. This is an especially great spot in the winter months.

You could say that the Detroit Zoo is an A+, since it exhibits animals from Australia, Africa, Asia, the Arctic, and the Antarctic. The outdoor exhibits are designed to give the animals room to wander and water to wade into at their pleasure. The buildings here tend to be reminiscent of older zoos, but sometimes such buildings are needed to help the animals escape the extremes of weather and to support the outdoor exhibits. The signs and placards are colorful and include stories of the people from the animals' homelands.

Make sure you stop by Amphibiville—a National Amphibian Conservation Center. It is a small exhibit building but will fascinate your grandkids with all the forms of life that we normally consider slimy and squirmy. A picture of a princess holding a frog at the entrance reminds us of the significance of these creatures in fairy tales, and highlights the symbolic connection of transformation and our ability to find the beautiful in the ugly.

Bonding & Bridging

When children see new animal species for the first time, the excitement is contagious and appeals to everyone. We're all fascinated by animals, especially those we may only have seen in television shows or movies. At the zoo we can marvel in safety at the grace and beauty of animals that are often scarce or endangered. Zoos let us talk about nature and the animals that live in the wild. Kids empathize with animals; they want to be good caretakers. We grandparents should nurture that empathy. Zoos give us a chance to talk about how we can help animals survive in the wild, which can be as simple as deciding what we buy in the grocery store, as habitat loss is the biggest threat to these animals. For older children there are the more difficult questions about issues of captivity. Is it right and, if so, why? We would also recommend that you talk to older children about the breeding programs that zoos have and how they are trying to save animal species that are disappearing in the wild.

A WORD TO THE WISE:
The Polk Penguin Center is a new feature of the zoo and should be especially popular on hot summer days. To enter this penguin haven you first have to walk into the building, which looks just like an iceberg; inside you'll find a crevasse, a waterfall, and king, gentoo, macaroni, and rockhopper penguins. With over 80 birds and 4-D effects built into the experience, you might have a hard time getting your grandkids to leave!

AGE OF GRANDCHILD: Toddler to teenager

BEST SEASON: Any season—but spring and early summer are best for seeing baby animals.

CONTACT: 8450 W 10 Mile Rd., Royal Oak, MI 48067; (248) 541-5717; www.detroitzoo.org

ALSO CHECK OUT:
Binder Park Zoo, Battle Creek: www.binderparkzoo.org

Children's Zoo at Celebration Square, Saginaw: www.saginawzoo.com

Garlyn Zoo, Naubinway (Upper Peninsula): www.garlynzoo.com

Potter Park Zoo, Lansing: www.potterparkzoo.org

One of the most powerful handclasps is that of a new grandbaby around the finger of a grandfather. JOY HARGROVE

Greenfield Village

Greenfield Village has been described as the oldest and largest outdoor museum in the U.S., but it's more like a historical theme park that pays particular attention to motorized vehicles. Part of "The Henry Ford," a museum complex that encompasses a number of different venues and exhibits, Greenfield Village was designed and built by Henry Ford himself. He created Greenfield Village in 1929 to preserve examples of American buildings and ways of life for future generations to appreciate.

This is a large village and it covers 80 acres, so ride in a Model T or a Model AA bus, or hop on the train to get around the site. There's no question, the grandkids will get a charge out of riding in these old-fashioned conveyances.

Many of the people Henry Ford admired are represented in the structures scattered throughout the village, and those structures include the Wright Brothers' Bike Shop, the Logan County Courthouse where Abe Lincoln tried cases, Edison's Menlo Park Laboratory, and George Washington Carver's cabin. Some of the buildings are originals and were moved to the site, including a seventeenth-century English cottage. Others are replicas that were built onsite.

In order to make the experience as real and educational as possible, skilled reenactors, some of whom are true artisans, are located throughout the Village and will gladly share information about their lives and their work. Potters, glass blowers, and farmers are just some of the occupations represented.

Grandkids will especially enjoy springtime when baby animals are plentiful at the farm. Younger grandkids will be drawn to the Herschell-Spillman Carousel with its hand-carved animals. Even some of the food served in the Village is based on authentic recipes from the 1800s. Because it is such a large site, it is probably best not to try to see all of it in one visit. Sore feet and frazzled feelings are likely to follow. There is also a small children's area where your grandchildren can engage in some supervised play, and it is a good place for a breather. They will like getting involved, and all of you will be ready to continue the exploration afterward.

Greenfield Village focuses on the accomplishments of Americans who believed in the dream that hard work and creative minds would bring personal success and benefit society as a whole. The Village creates the sense of optimism of the "good ol' days." Henry Ford is an example of the American spirit that epitomized our second century. We want to encourage our grandchildren to be hard-working and productive members of society, to understand the need for civic involvement and regional pride. We also know that they are going to be the ones who will have to create new technologies and pathways for a future that looks especially challenging. As you visit the various workshops, talk to the grandkids about how different working conditions are today than they were 100 years ago. What do they see Americans doing or creating in this century? Just as Henry Ford created the Model T, if your grandchildren keep searching for better solutions, they have the potential to change the world.

A WORD TO THE WISE:

While any time is a good time to visit Greenfield Village, there are a few occasions that may provide you and the grandchildren a more fun and focused visit. From June through August you can watch baseball played as it was in the late 1800s and early 1900s. They have a Halloween program that runs Friday–Sunday nights called "Hallowe'en in Greenfield Village." In December there's a program on select nights called "Holiday Nights in Greenfield Village."

AGE OF GRANDCHILD: Toddler to teenager

BEST SEASON: Any season—but spring and early summer are best for seeing baby animals.

CONTACT: The Henry Ford, 20900 Oakwood Blvd., Dearborn, MI 48124-5029; (313) 982-6001, (800) 835-5237; www.thehenryford.org/visit/greenfield-village

ALSO CHECK OUT:

Crossroads Village & Huckleberry Railroad, Flint: http://geneseecountyparks.org/crossroads%20village/

Mackinac Island: www.mackinacisland.org

They say genes skip generations. Maybe that's why grandparents find their grandchildren so likeable. JOAN MCINTOSH

Henry Ford Museum

This museum is dedicated to the history of the Ford Plant, Henry Ford, and the automobile, and is known as "The Henry Ford"—this is simple and all that needs to be said. Henry Ford is a national icon, but he holds a special place in Detroit and its history. He did not invent the automobile; that was done by Gottlieb Daimler and Karl Benz, but he popularized the assembly line, which helped make the automobile universal and affordable.

The museum is lodged in a large and magnificent facility that was created as a showplace for history, and it is so encompassing that you want to allow yourself a lot of time to explore. Old diners and road signs help set the mood and provide you with artifacts from different eras and their context. The automobile is featured, of course; we come here because of it, but you

won't find just Ford products. There are vehicles from past presidents, motorcycles, classic cars, as well as unique and wild designs that are humorous and informative. We found an old racer like the one Mike's grandfather drove, and we loved the look of the original campers, including the one Charles Lindbergh used.

These are all arranged neatly, in a progressive parade over time, or in clusters that represent a design era. Often the signs and support materials are as fun as the vehicle, but you have to make sure that you slow down enough to check them out. There is also a film section where you can find a bench and enjoy a movie or part of one. There are railroad cars and even stagecoaches on one side of the cars, as well as an excellent airplane exhibit that features Ford's history in aviation. This includes stories and aircraft. Ford's relationship to invention and industry is well exhibited, too. "Made in America" is a celebration of the industrial revolution in the United States and inventors like Ford's good friend, Thomas Edison.

There is also a small children's area where your grandchildren can engage in some supervised play, and it is a good place for a breather. They will like getting involved, and all of you will be ready to continue the exploration afterward.

The museum has an excellent display for making connections between generations; it is called "Your Place in Time" and there is a section devoted to each decade in the twentieth century. You can go to your time and show the grandchildren what you had and what people were doing during your childhood; then you can go to their parents' decade and help them see the change before visiting their own decade. This is the most visual and fun way we have found to make time travel happen.

As you travel from your decade to theirs, make sure they know you have experienced all of them in between. You've been part of the changes, and their life will also be one of change and opportunity.

A WORD TO THE WISE:

Get your hand stamped so you can enter and exit at your own pace. Kids have a set attention span, and they will move from place to place throughout the museum. But they also need a break from the stimuli—so take a walk outside, catch a movie at the Giant Screen Experience. It is OK to go in and out, but be sure to check out the Weinermobile, where people used to buy food to eat. Be prepared to linger at certain exhibits, some pertinent to the grandparent and others to grandchildren. Look for a nice balance.

AGE OF GRANDCHILD: 3 and up

BEST SEASON: All seasons, but summer if you want Greenfield Village, too.

CONTACT: The Henry Ford, 20900 Oakwood Blvd., Dearborn, MI 48124-5029; (313) 982-6001, (800) 835-5237; www.thehenryford.org/visit; check out the special online exhibits, too

ALSO CHECK OUT:

Alfred P. Sloan Museum, Flint: www.sloanlongway.org/about-sloan

Automotive Hall of Fame, Dearborn: www.automotivehalloffame.org

Gilmore Car Museum, Hickory Corners: www.gilmorecarmuseum.org

GM Heritage Center, Sterling Heights: www.gmheritagecenter.com

R. E. Olds Transportation Museum: www.reoldsmuseum.org

If a child is to keep alive his inborn sense of wonder, he needs the companionship of at least one adult who can share it, rediscovering with him the joy, excitement and mystery of the world we live in. RACHEL CARSON

Ford Rouge Factory Tour

It was 48 years between visits to the Rouge Plant for Mike, and according to him, it is the same location but not the same place. This begs the question, What will it look like if our grandchildren return in 48 more years?

Mike remembers hot molten metal and the dark interior, but it doesn't look like that now. Catch the bus at The Henry Ford, and the short ride, with narration from the driver, will connect you with the other Ford facilities and stories. When you arrive, be prepared for a multisensory experience. The first event is in a theater where you watch a film that gives you historic perspective. It is short, which is good, because this can test the younger grandchildren. The second theater alleviates any boredom that might be setting in.

The Henry Ford describes its newest theater like this, "The reimagined Manufacturing Innovation Theater, designed by BRC Imagination Arts, immerses visitors into the world of actual production—from concept to final testing—through state-of-the-art special effects including 3-D projection mapping, laser effects and actual moving robots."

You will exit and move to the production line. None of the theaters were here on Mike's first visit, but then again, the construction line was not like this either. Colorful stations, color-coded parts, men and women in chairs that

move them into the right position in a healthy way, and a pickup coming together as it moves from station to station. No smoky conditions, no dirt, the workers are clean and protected thanks to the work of their unions—another story that unfolds in this experience. It is a good walk around the assembly plant, and it is worth taking your time, talking, and pointing. This part of the tour is self-guided, with video support in some sections and posters in others. Next is the observation deck, an overview of the massive factory complex and the new, important designs created to lessen the impact on the environment—green roofs with growing plants to filter the air and absorb carbon, plus rain gardens and wetlands to catch runoff from the large parking lots.

This place created the modern car and the city of Detroit. Located on the Rouge River, the plant has assembled more vehicles than we could count. It is the result of one man's dream; he brought the raw materials to the workers, who assembled them into the Model T, and this led to everything that followed.

Bonding & Bridging

Cars exist all over the world, but nowhere else have they been more important to a culture. We have grown up in our parents' cars, anticipated being handed the keys for the first time, and we cherished the first time we pulled out of the driveway on our own. This has been a twentieth-century rite of passage. From roadsters to Mustangs to hybrids, we've seen our vehicles change and advance according to the demands of the buyer. Share your car stories, or tell them about your dream car; this can be fun for the grandchildren if you allow them to choose theirs as well. What color do you like? A convertible? A pickup? Economy or luxury? Choices need to be made and each decision is important. Start here and examine how and why we choose what we do.

A WORD TO THE WISE:

This tour is part of the three major options that include The Henry Ford Museum and Greenfield Village, but we recommend you treat each of these as a separate visit, if that is possible in your schedule. As you have probably figured out if you have read many of our recommendations, it is better to do too little than too much. When grandchildren melt down because of exhaustion, overstimulation, or frustration, it ruins everyone's day. When grandparents get too tired, frustrated, physically exhausted, and short tempered or grumpy, it also ruins the whole day. So the compromise is to take experiences in shorter, more controlled segments. Go to the hotel or home, go to a park and let the grandchildren play, and then come back the next day for another experience.

AGE OF GRANDCHILD: 5 and up

BEST SEASON: Any

CONTACT: The Henry Ford, 20900 Oakwood Blvd., Dearborn, MI 48124-5029; (313) 982-6001, (800) 835-5237; www.thehenryford.org/visit/ford-rouge-factory-tour

ALSO CHECK OUT:

GM Truck Assembly, Flint: http://flintassembly.gm.com/Facilities/public/us/en/flint/news.html

Forget not that the Earth delights to feel your bare feet, and the winds long to play with your hair. KAHLIL GIBRAN

Dossin Great Lakes Museum

Located near downtown Detroit on historic Belle Isle, this museum celebrates the maritime traditions of the Great Lakes, including the region's long history of shipping and outdoor recreation. Located amid a bottleneck for Great Lakes ship traffic, the museum is a great place to explore the area's unique nautical heritage.

The museum is home to a permanent exhibit called "Built by the River," which highlights how Detroit prospered and grew as a result of its relationship with the Detroit River. Known as the "City of Straits," Detroit has long been

an important crossroads. It was a focal point for everything from the fur trade to shipbuilding, and it was also a strategic military position for the French, and later, the British. In the twentieth century, it was even a center for illegal smuggling during Prohibition.

The museum gets its name from Michigan's famous Dossin family, which is known for its long ties to the PepsiCo company, and its longtime interest in the Great Lakes, especially hydroplanes. The family is represented at the museum by their famous hydroplane, Miss Pepsi, which once exceeded 100 miles per hour.

The museum also houses the ornate must-see "Gothic Room," which was the gentleman's room on the *City of Detroit III,* the pilot house from the SS *William Clay Ford,* artifacts from the *Edmund Fitzgerald,* and outdoor exhibits from other well-known Great Lakes ships, including those that participated in the Battle of Lake Erie in 1812.

Bonding & Bridging

Combine a visit to the museum with a walk along the Detroit River. The Great Lakes surround the state of Michigan, and are world treasures, but it is important to talk about just how essential water is in our lives. In the museum it is easy to see how it faciliated transportation, but what does water mean to your grandchild? How do they use it? Help them explore their own connection to freshwater, and through this gentle discovery you can help them to understand why freshwater is so precious and needs to be protected.

A WORD TO THE WISE:

The Richard and Jane Manoogian Ship Model Showcase is a revolving exhibit of model ships on display at the museum. Sometimes it is easier for children to explore their world through models that bring the huge boats into perspective. There are over 150 models here, and they date back over many decades. Most grandparents will remember making models at home, a hobby that has diminished in the age of electronics. These classic boats might even inspire a little model-making back home.

AGE OF GRANDCHILD: 5 and up

BEST SEASON: Any

CONTACT: 100 Strand Dr., Belle Isle, Detroit, MI 48207; (313) 833-5538; http://detroithistorical.org/dossin-great-lakes-museum/plan-your-visit/general-information

ALSO CHECK OUT:

Great Lakes Shipwreck Museum: www.shipwreckmuseum.com

Icebreaker *Mackinaw* Maritime Museum: www.themackinaw.org

Michigan Maritime Museum: www.michiganmaritimemuseum.org

A child is the greatest poem ever known. CHRISTOPHER MORLEY

Abbott Magic Company

Do you believe in magic? For this baby boomer grandma, that sentence immediately brings the music of the Lovin' Spoonful to mind. But for many children, especially the younger ones, that question will elicit a resounding "Yes!" For grandparents, magic brings up images of men in black capes pulling rabbits out of hats or quarters out of ears, all at the flick of a magic wand. For our grandchildren, magic is a boy in wire-rimmed glasses who lives in a fully magical world.

In Michigan, there is a place—a town—whose whole image is based on magic. Colon calls itself "The Magic Capital of the World." Here in this southwest corner of the state, far from the busy roads of commerce, is the town where magician Harry Blackstone chose to live from 1926 to 1949. He was followed

by another magician from Australia named Percy Abbott. They performed together for a while, but after a falling out over a business agreement, they went their separate ways. Abbott stayed in Colon, opened the Abbott Magic Company with a partner and continued to build the town's reputation as the Magic Capital.

The town has embraced the magic theme. Even the big concrete flower planters on the main street are designed to look like hats with rabbits coming out of the top. The town has designed and hopes to open a new city park that incorporates designs taken from magic tricks into its layout and structure.

Abbott Magic Company is still in operation, run by the son of Abbott's partner. The building itself sits on a side street and has seen better days. Inside, it is a combination of museum and store, filled from floor to ceiling with magic memorabilia, as well as goods for sale. Even the ceiling is plastered with old posters from magic shows of old. In the glass cases that circle the room, everyone from the very beginner to the professional can find something to suit their skills. There is another magic store in town on the main street, the Fab Magic Company, that has a more open feeling. Both offer Saturday afternoon magic shows in the summer months.

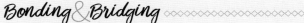

Bonding & Bridging

You've been performing magic for your grandchildren ever since you played peekaboo with them. So many day-to-day activities we take for granted seem like magic to children, and we love the wonder on their faces—probably because it reminds us of when we were innocent. Curiosity is stimulated by magic, too. As we grow older we want to know how the magician does his tricks. Card tricks may be the easiest to learn, although you may need to buy a special deck of cards. If your grandchildren show an interest in this hobby, enter into it with them and encourage their early efforts. If there is a popular magician performing near you, make a date with your grandchild to see the show together. Lance Burton, a famous magician, went to his first magic show at age 6 and was hooked for life. Whether this interest continues or fades with time, they will know that we all need a little magic in our lives.

A WORD TO THE WISE:

The Abbott Magic Company and the Fab Magic Company both offer weekend magic shows at their stores, but the real magic happens in the summer when the town celebrates Magic Week and the great Magic Get Together. This extravaganza brings in performing magicians—and audiences—from throughout the country. The special children's show happens during the Saturday matinee. In addition, the town of Marshall has the American Museum of Magic. It is easy to combine this museum with a visit to Colon and provide even more connections with magic. The magic museum is a personal collection assembled by a man who raised over 18,000 doves for magicians to use in their acts!

AGE OF GRANDCHILD: 3 to teenager

BEST SEASON: Summer

CONTACT: 124 Joseph St., Colon, MI 49040; (269) 432-3235; www.abbottmagic.com

ALSO CHECK OUT:

American Museum of Magic, Marshall: www.americanmuseumofmagic.com

Fab Magic Company, Colon: www.fabmagic.com

A child needs a grandparent, anybody's grandparent, to grow a little more securely into an unfamiliar world. **CHARLES AND ANN MORSE**

Air Zoo

Flying stirs our souls and our imaginations. We are bird watchers because we envy the freedom our avian friends have in flight. Our dreams of flying are often some of our most memorable, and we have tried to make those dreams a reality since the beginning of time. So it is no wonder that this wonderful collection of flying vehicles, which includes everything from primitive flight to vehicles used for space exploration, is such a great hit with people of all ages.

Here, you can explore technology and learn how it has impacted our culture with real hands-on experiences; there is a Guadalcanal exhibit that provides insights into World War II. The Montgolfier balloon ride, along with the flying circus biplane ride, take you back in time—but even more remarkable,

you can have a flight in a real biplane. Or you can get into the flight simulator, where your stability and motion tolerance will be tested. If that is not enough, you can get into a 3-D simulation of the space shuttle and take off into space.

There is the 4-D movie theater that combines 3-D with movable seats, surround sound, live actors, and computer simulations that will leave you wondering if you experienced a real World War II bombing mission or just had the strongest dream you will ever experience.

Explore the collection of vintage and current aircraft arranged in appropriate combinations with mannequins dressed for the era and scene. Some planes are ominous and seem alive; others are almost comical in their simplicity and historic design.

Then you can wander to the other campus where one of the rooms explores space flight. Kids can strap into a harness and see what it would feel like to walk on the moon or check out the displays that show the food, the first aid, and even the toilet of the astronaut's space home. The Air Zoo also features the Michigan Space Science Center, which includes a Mission to Mars experience and space artifacts.

All in all, there is a variety of airplanes inside and outside. Each represents a time, a place, and a story; together they represent the timeline of aviation and the quest for the ultimate liftoff.

Bonding & Bridging ⟩⟨⟩⟨⟩⟨⟩⟨⟩⟨⟩⟨⟩⟨⟩⟨⟩⟨⟩⟨⟩⟨⟩⟨⟩⟨⟩⟨⟩⟨

The Air Zoo has many ways to explore and learn, but if you have a grand-child aged 9–15 you should consider participating in one of the Homeschool Discovery Days at the Air Zoo, offered during the school year from September to May. The programs are hands-on and the instructors will help you explore aviation, space, science, or history. The sessions are three and a half hours long and will give you something to discuss and share while helping children develop their science knowledge and skills.

Super Science Saturdays are another option for making science entertaining and unforgettable. Math, science, and nature taught by enthusiastic leaders in an active and fun setting are more ways to share and grow together.

A WORD TO THE WISE:

It is easy to get caught up in the high technology of military jets and the adventure of space exploration, but help your grandchildren get the full picture by teaching them about the early forms of flight as well. Build their knowledge by building a model plane or flying a kite. Our grandchildren love the simple balsa gliders and love that they can actually make something fly. There are many models available, from simple planes with the slip-in balsa wing to elaborate radio-controlled airplanes. Choose the one that fits your budget and your interest and follow up on this flight of fancy.

AGE OF GRANDCHILD: 3 and up

BEST SEASON: A nice inside escape on a cold winter day.

CONTACT: 6151 Portage Rd., Portage, MI 49002; (269) 382-6555; www.airzoo.org

ALSO CHECK OUT:

Frankenmuth, Michigan's own military and space museum: www.michigansmilitarymuseum.com

Selfridge Military Air Museum: www.selfridgeairmuseum.org

Yankee Air Museum: www.yankeeairmuseum.org

I like to walk with Grandpa, his steps are short like mine.
He doesn't say, "Now hurry up." He always takes his time. Unknown

Kalamazoo Nature Center

As culture becomes more complex, we often lose the sense of place that was part of our ancestors' world. People used to connect with the land out of necessity through farming, logging, hunting, and fishing.

We have turned to industry and cities, and have become separated from the source of our food, oxygen, and water. Naturalists offered people insight through their writings and encouraged people to find inspiration and renewal by visiting natural areas, but this became a problem as the land became more

and more developed. Around the time of the original Earth Day in 1970, the concept of the nature center took off, but the Kalamazoo Nature Center dates back to the 1950s and is one of the landmarks in environmental education and history.

Kalamazoo Nature Center is located in Cooper's Glen, a historically significant natural area connected to human history, as well as to the natural history of the region.

It was preserved because of Dr. H. Lewis Batts, Jr., who helped make this a nature preserve. Its 1,100 acres of wooded, rolling countryside five miles north of Kalamazoo are a real treasure, a gift for today and for the future.

Nature centers, unlike parks, were designed in neighborhoods and in the country specifically to educate visitors about the environment. They emphasize forests, lakes, rivers, or prairies. But most importantly, they remind us that no matter how many stores we have, the basic goods still come from the Earth, and we need the clean air and water that nature provides.

You approach the Visitor Center on an elevated walkway, through trees and above a ravine, which allows you to become part of the landscape. Inside, you walk through a botanical rainforest display, and there is a set of comfortable chairs for watching the bird feeders, as well as displays, animals, classes, and a wonderful set of hosts who will help you get involved and comfortable immediately.

Then you can go outside, walk the trails, explore the woods, watch the birds, and find the spaces where your spirit and your grandchildren can be inspired.

Many nature centers have benches where you can watch birds feed or look out on the forest, lake, or wetland. These are good places for grandparent-to-grandchild sharing. What do they think nature is? Do they think people are part of nature? What makes a place special? How does this place look to a bird or mammal? Is nature around their home, and if so, can they watch it and enjoy it? What are the lessons they learned from visiting the nature center? What is it that they really liked? Would they want to be naturalists when they grow up, like the people who work at the nature center? There are no correct answers for these questions. Sometimes our conversations put questions in the grandchild's mind. They will come back to them when the time is right.

A WORD TO THE WISE:

A nature center is a part of your neighborhood, like a store, an office building, or a home. This implies that nature should be part of our community. Humans need to learn to live with other life-forms, just as they adapt to the changes in our local setting. Ask your grandchildren who lived here first. Ask them if they like the birds at the feeders and the things that live at the nature center. Building a good future for our grandchildren means allowing nature to have a role in our human communities. Take advantage of the Sunday afternoon family programs to continue to explore nature and the connection with people.

AGE OF GRANDCHILD: All

BEST SEASON: Spring has the most life!

CONTACT: 7000 N Westnedge Ave., Kalamazoo, MI 49009; (269) 381-1574; www.naturecenter.org

ALSO CHECK OUT:

Chippewa Nature Center: www.chippewanaturecenter.org

DeGraaf Nature Center: www.cityofholland.com/degraafnaturecenter

List of Michigan Nature Centers:
www.michigan.gov/deq/0,1607,7-135-3307_3580-107287--,00.html

Michigan Audubon Sanctuaries:
www.michiganaudubon.org/our-conservation-impact/bird-sanctuaries/

Everyone needs to have access both to grandparents and grandchildren in order to be a full human being. MARGARET MEAD

Holland Tulips

Picture this: boulevards of tulips in the spring sunshine, hand-crafted wooden shoes made in a local factory, and a windmill turning in the breeze over the water. Now where are you? Of course, you are in Holland—Holland, Michigan, that is.

The annual Tulip Time Festival is one of the most popular events in Michigan and is in keeping with its heritage and name. The town's founder, a man named Albertus Van Raalte, came to the shores of Lake Michigan in the 1800s seeking to create a community that represented his roots and aspirations. This was not easy in frontier Michigan, and his efforts were really set back in 1871 when a fire nearly destroyed all but two structures, which still stand today.

For Northerners, spring flowers and migrating birds satisfy a longing for color. In winter, we live in a white-and-brown world with only pine trees to color our horizons. The days are short, the nights are cold, and we have developed expressions like "cabin fever" and "seasonal affective disorder" to describe our mood, so imagine 4.5 million tulips in one community!

When the bulbs burst through the soil, the green stalks rise above the ground, and the buds burst with color, it is time to celebrate. The Tulip Time Festival features parades, music, food, entertainers, and concerts like most community celebrations, but here there are some added experiences.

Visit the Veldheer Tulip Gardens where you can walk among the acres of blooms and glimpse the beauty of European Holland. Then you can visit the Deklomp Wooden Shoe and Delft Factory where artists mold, glaze, and hand-paint the blue-and-white pottery, and where you can see wooden shoes created on the Dutch carving machines! These are unique products and processes. The Nelis' Dutch Village is another location with a shoe shop, carousel, and Dutch-style buildings. It features klompen dancers (they wear wooden shoes!) and music from a towering 25-bell carillon.

You can also go to the Windmill Island Gardens to see the only authentic Dutch windmill operating in the U.S.; it is 250 years old. There are gardens, dikes, and canals, as well as a hand-painted Dutch carousel. Allow yourself to settle into this mini-European vacation. More than 100,000 tulips bloom here in the spring! The island also includes a miniature Dutch village.

Bonding & Bridging

Explore your heritage and help your grandchildren understand where their ancestors came from and how connected we really are to the world. Visit these sites and enjoy these experiences for their contrast with what we experience on the average day, but also honor the customs of other cultures and what they represent.

See if you can challenge the grandchildren to be brave and taste the *erwtensoep* (pea soup), metworst (beef sausage) or a speculaasje (spiced cookie), and then seek out the storyteller at the gazebo in Centennial Park to complete your ethnic sampler.

A WORD TO THE WISE:

Do not look for a Dutch village—this is a village with a Dutch background. If you come to enjoy the celebration and engage in the events, you will have a wonderful time; but if you are expecting a quaint village that is straight off the canvas of a Dutch master, you will be disappointed. Sometimes we have to work to keep expectations grounded in reality, or we lose the options that we do find. Brochures, even our text, can start your imagination rolling. Remember that all the materials we look at are designed to sell an idea or a location. What is important here is the fun that is offered, the chance to play and celebrate spring, enjoy a bite of Dutch chocolate, and have a good attitude.

AGE OF GRANDCHILD: 3 and up

BEST SEASON: Spring

CONTACT: Holland Tulip Time Festival: www.tuliptime.com

Nelis' Dutch Village: www.dutchvillage.com

Veldheer Tulip Gardens: www.veldheer.com

Windmill Island Gardens: www.cityofholland.com/windmillislandgardens

ALSO CHECK OUT:

Bavarian celebrations at Frankenmuth: www.frankenmuth.org

Heikinpaiva at Hancock: www.cityofhancock.com

Scottish heritage, Alma: www.almahighlandfestival.com

Grandmas are moms with lots of frosting. UNKNOWN

Butterfly Gardens

How many of us have put a monarch caterpillar into an empty mayonnaise jar with some milkweed leaves and watched it turn into a chrysalis and then emerge as a butterfly? This is a miraculous sight for a person of any age, but especially for a child. Butterflies have always fascinated us because of their fragility, their colorful patterns, and their ability to float effortlessly in the air. Some, like the monarchs, are capable of vast journeys, which seems impossible for such a wisp of creation. While zoos and aquariums are familiar places to see wildlife, butterfly gardens and houses have become increasingly popular. Now people can come face-to-face with a vast variety of species from the tropics, as well as those native to temperate life zones.

There are two exceptional locations in Michigan to see butterflies. Both are in buildings with tropical plants and water, which make them especially inviting during the last stages of winter or early spring. The largest temporary butterfly display is found at the Frederik Meijer Gardens & Sculpture Park in Grand Rapids. Here, each March and April, butterflies drift and float by in the 15,000-square-foot conservatory. A special Butterfly Bungalow holds hundreds of chrysalides (cocoons) behind glass; there, you can see the variation in their shapes, sizes, and colors. You may also have the chance to see a butterfly

emerge from its cocoon. Special dishes hold nectar, and butterflies gather on these, as well as on flowers and puddles of water throughout the bungalow.

At the Detroit Zoo in the Wildlife Interpretive Gallery, you can watch butterflies as they seek nectar from flowers and ripe fruit. In order to prevent the accidental introduction of non-native butterfly species into our country, there are no plants in the building on which they can lay eggs. All of these butterflies arrive at the zoo in chrysalis form at the zoo from special breeders in Costa Rica and El Salvador and live for approximately two weeks, which is longer than their normal life span in the wild. Besides the butterflies, there are several hummingbirds living among the vegetation, another magnificent example of nature's creativity. Docents at both places are ready to answer questions about the butterflies and the hummingbirds.

Bonding & Bridging

Butterflies are the embodiment of change and can be metaphors for so much. It can be as hard for our grandchildren to imagine that we once were their size and age, as it is difficult for them to imagine a caterpillar becoming a butterfly. For older grandchildren, understanding this metamorphosis may be especially difficult, as they might feel trapped in the cocoon of childhood, but yearn to be free. Talk to them about difficult changes you have endured in your life. After visiting a butterfly garden, you can plant a butterfly garden of your own. The website www.butterfly--garden.com can help you figure out what plants are most suitable for caterpillars and later, butterflies.

A WORD TO THE WISE:

It is a great temptation to grab, pet, or touch a butterfly that lands nearby. This is not allowed in any of the locations, because the insect's fragile wings can be easily damaged. This will be a challenge to explain to toddlers, so keep a close watch. If a butterfly chooses to land on one of you, just enjoy the gift. It will fly away soon enough. Because this is a temporary exhibit, it will be very crowded on weekends, and you may want to try to visit on a weekday, if at all possible.

AGE OF GRANDCHILD: Toddler to teenager

BEST SEASON: Springtime—just before the butterflies begin to return to our gardens and yards.

CONTACT: Detroit Zoo: 8450 W Ten Mile Rd., Royal Oak, MI 48067; (248) 541-5717; www.detroitzoo.org/animal-habitat/butterfly-garden

Frederik Meijer Gardens & Sculpture Park: 1000 E Beltline Ave. NE, Grand Rapids, MI 49525; (616) 957-1580, (888) 957-1580; www.meijergardens.org/calendar/butterflies-are-blooming/

ALSO CHECK OUT:

Mackinac Island Butterfly House and Insect World: www.originalbutterflyhouse.com

Michigan State University Butterfly House, East Lansing: http://4hgarden.cowplex.com/Butterflies

One hundred years from now, it will not matter what my bank account was, how big my house was, or what kind of car I drove. But the world may be a little better because I was important in the life of a child. Forest Witcraft

Lena Meijer Children's Garden at Frederik Meijer Gardens & Sculpture Park

Who would ever imagine that a garden could be exciting and fun for kids? Too many generations, including our own, have grown up associating the word "garden" with being down on your knees pulling weeds in the hot sun. The Lena Meijer Children's Garden in Grand Rapids turns the word "garden" into a playground full of discovery for all the senses. The kids will know immediately that someone was thinking about them when they see the miniature gate they can duck through, like a magical mouse hole into another world.

The Kid-Sense Garden has a combination of sculptures, including an eye, ear, and a tongue that clue the visitor in to the plants growing nearby. Here you can touch, sniff, and even taste some of the flowers, leaves, and fruits. Playground Activity Leaders (PALS) are on hand to introduce you to these sensory delights. The Great Lakes are represented by raised pools that allow hand-splashing. A Storytelling Garden with a stage and storytelling hut allows the kids to use their imaginations and create stories or skits using what they see around them. A boardwalk takes you through a natural wetland, where red-winged blackbirds sing from cattails, and on to a giant sandbox area known as the "Quarry" where kids can dig for fossils or just create sand and stone sculptures like those scattered all over the property. Nearby is a Log Cabin with a table and a checkerboard game ready to play. Benches and a fireplace give the building an authentic feel. Next it's on to a series of elevated tree houses that feel like a Robinson Crusoe creation. The suspended bridges between each house give an adventurous touch. Small, fixed spotting scopes are here and along the trail, with clues about what to look for. A labyrinth and hedge-lined maze will give the kids a way to slow down as you leave the garden area.

Children should not touch or climb the sculptures throughout this five-acre garden. This will be a temptation—especially with the dragon sculpture. Make sure the kids study the Wolf Pack, created with recycled materials. This may just inspire them to think of ways they can reuse or recycle some of their own toys. Stop at the Information Building near the entrance/exit. Here they can do crafts or settle down to read a book related to gardening or other special exhibits featured during the year.

Bonding & Bridging

Visiting a children's garden can be the starting point for a lifetime love of plants. It can also be the starting point for joint ventures with you and the grandchildren. Whether you live in a city apartment or on a country estate, together you can plan and plant a garden. Think about making Earth Day in April your starting date. Attend special Earth Day events here or at other venues, and then visit a garden center or nursery to see what you might want to plant. April is a bit early for most places in Michigan to put plants in the ground, but you can get some ideas and then go back home and make a diagram or drawing of what your garden will look like. You can also start some seeds indoors, and every time your grandchildren visit they can see the changes, until finally they can help you transplant the seedlings into the garden. Document this project with lots of photos from start to finish, when you harvest the first tomatoes together.

A WORD TO THE WISE:

Of course, the most wonderful time to visit this garden is in the summer when everything is in bloom with color and scents, but don't shun it in the fall and early spring, once the snow is gone. It's good for kids to understand the variations that come with gardening, how a garden fades away and lies dormant in preparation for a new season. Special winter activities include animal tracking and bird watching, and you won't have crowds to compete with for the space.

AGE OF GRANDCHILD: Toddler to 10

BEST SEASON: Summer

CONTACT: 1000 E Beltline Ave. NE, Grand Rapids, MI 49525; (616) 957-1580, (888) 957-1580; www.meijergardens.org/attractions/childrens-garden/

ALSO CHECK OUT:

4-H Children's Garden at Michigan State University, East Lansing: 4hgarden.cowplex.com

Leila Arboretum, Battle Creek: www.lasgarden.org

Never have children, only grandchildren. Gore Vidal

Michigan History Museum

History is an aspect of this book that pops up time and again. Why? Because studying and celebrating history is an important step toward understanding ourselves. Fortunately, teaching our grandchildren about Michigan history is not a difficult task. There is evidence of this great state's past all around us. To make it even easier, the Michigan History Museum in Lansing is filled with beautiful, colorful, and fascinating exhibits to enlighten all ages. The museum opened in 1989 and covers the history of the state from prehistoric times up through the last half of the twentieth century. In the light-filled, glass-walled atrium, you are presented with a three-story-high topographic map on the wall, showing in great detail how the glaciers carved the land known today as Michigan. This will give you a sense of how the natural history influenced human history.

There are four levels, 26 permanent galleries, and more information and artifacts than any person can absorb in just one visit. Decide in advance to do just two levels and then really take your time to study and enjoy the exhibits. The galleries have many glassed-in displays showing tools and everyday objects from the time of the Paleo-Indians through the settlement period and into

the industrialization period of the 1900s. But there are also many beautiful, lifelike dioramas that feel as though you could step into the scene and feel the grasses and the breeze blowing past.

You will probably have the most fun in the 1950s gallery where you can walk through an exhibit designed to look like a 1957 auto show. You may find yourself "oohing" and "aahing" over the shiny, finned classic cars, including a candy-red Corvette. You can design your own concept car on a computer. The other part of this gallery that will create nostalgia for many is the 1950s home. You can explain to your grandkids that these artifacts and furnishings were like those you had or used when you were a child. The same can be said for the 1960s gallery; chances are good, you will all be laughing at some of the clothing and other modern conveniences of those times. Ask the kids what things they use or own that will someday be considered funny or old-fashioned. Kids especially enjoy imagining what the future will be like.

Bonding & Bridging

How many of us remember yawning in history class or daydreaming when that subject came up? This generation of grandchildren is no different from us, but a good museum can create excitement and curiosity about the past in a way that the classroom never can.

Every one of us has a personal history and when it's personal, it is always more interesting. Talk with your grandchildren about events that have been important to them. Was it the first day of school, the holidays, the house they moved to? Then tell them some of the important parts of your history, but not so that their eyes glaze over. Encourage them to write about their daily lives—whether in a diary or journal, or in emails to you—which you then print out and save for them. One never knows how the events that we record today might someday be of interest to the future generations.

A WORD TO THE WISE:

The museum is home to a wide variety of displays and exhibits, and they range from *The Arsenal of Democracy,* which discusses the pivotal role Detroit played in supplying the Allies during World War II to exhibits about Michigan's long history with the mining and lumber industries. There's even a speakeasy and a 1920s-themed hallway!

AGE OF GRANDCHILD: 7 to teenager

BEST SEASON: All

CONTACT: 702 W Kalamazoo St., Lansing MI 48915; (517) 373-3559; www.michigan.gov/mhc

ALSO CHECK OUT:

Detroit Historical Museum: https://detroithistorical.org/detroit-historical-museum/plan-your-visit/general-information

Children are like windows that open onto the future as well as the past, the external world as well as our own private landscapes. JANE SWIGART

Michigan State Capitol

We are a culture of symbols—religious, economic, and political—and perhaps no structure is more symbolic of our democratic system than a state capitol. The Michigan State Capitol is modeled after the United States Capitol and

designed by an architect named Elijah E. Myers, who designed three state capitol buildings (more than any other architect)! The building was completed in 1879.

This is not Michigan's first capitol building. Like most states, the early governments were not in a position to create a suitable building; their efforts had to go into building a state first. And like other states, even the capital city changed. The state's first capital was Detroit, but in 1847 it moved from Detroit to Lansing for two reasons: there was a need for the state to spread out to the west, and there was the potential threat of the British troops in Windsor. In Lansing, the first capitol structure was a frame house that served until a better building could be made. The first capitol building became a school until it burned in 1893. The second capitol was white with green shutters, and it became a factory after the legislature moved out. Like the first capitol, it disappeared in flames.

Following the Civil War, the new capitols became monuments to the national government and the symbolism was repeated from state to state. The interior was an expression of the higher ideals of humanity, and decorative paintings were used so extensively that the capitol literally became a museum of decorative arts.

It is hard not to be impressed by a building that incorporates so much power and wealth, and your grandchildren will be impressed by the dome, the large-scale art, the open stairways, the center rotunda, and the paintings of past governors.

Look into the chambers where laws are passed, go into the galleries if they are in session, and watch the messy process from the balcony. Stroll the halls, find your senators, and go next door to find your representatives. You can wander on your own, but there are regular tours given every day. Groups must make reservations in advance.

The lesson you can impart from your own history is that it is the people who make a difference in this country. The building is in essence yours. These are your employees, and it is your responsibility to make sure they are doing a good job, or you vote them out. Is there any more important lesson we can impart to our grandchildren? Democracy works only when individuals make their voices heard.

Ask your grandchildren what they think is important in the country and help them draft a letter to their senators or representatives. Show them how to participate in government.

Here is the place to begin. Tell stories—share history. Take another walk around the grounds after the tour. Find out who we thought was significant enough to have a statue, visit the war memorials, visit the legislative and the judicial branches, and go to the Lansing museums.

A WORD TO THE WISE:

Make an appointment to visit your senators and representatives. Even if you know them at home, they look different in their offices. Get a photo taken. Be prepared with a few good questions so the conversation doesn't lag, but do not make this a lobbying visit. If they are not in a committee or session, they love to see their constituents—especially when you are not there to lobby or complain! And they especially like to see young people showing an interest in our government.

AGE OF GRANDCHILD: 12 and up

BEST SEASON: The most excitement and energy is when the legislature is in session.

CONTACT: 100 N Capitol Ave., Lansing, MI 48933; (517) 373-0184; http://capitol.michigan.gov

ALSO CHECK OUT:

Gerald R. Ford Presidential Library & Museum: www.fordlibrarymuseum.gov

Library of Michigan, Lansing: www.michigan.gov/libraryofmichigan

Grandma always made you feel she had been waiting to see just you all day and now the day was complete. MARCY DeMAREE

Festival Fun in Frankenmuth

We all love to pretend, and there is nothing better than a good stage set and a well-planned party to bring out the kid in both adults and children. Sometimes amusement or theme parks try to give us this make-believe pleasure, but they tend to be too confined to convince what we are experiencing could be real.

Fortunately for the playful family and the adventurous explorer, there is Frankenmuth—the Bavarian community in Michigan. The central city area has retained its character and stayed true to its "Chamber of Commerce" mission, while the rest of the community grows into the twenty-first century.

A long time ago some civic leaders recognized that a city could be successful even if it didn't border the Great Lakes or a major river and that not having a major industry could be an advantage. It meant the city could concentrate on

having fun. These civic leaders looked back to their founders for inspiration. Founded in 1845 by 15 German Lutheran missionaries who came to meet the Ojibwa, Frankenmuth built on its German (Bavarian) origins, and the real story of this storybook town is the number of festivals it hosts.

The area hosts many different festivals, all throughout the year. Frankenmuth offers quite a range of experiences, too— from colonial encampments where you can meet reenactors at French, American or English camps, to huge car shows, the Scarecrow Festival in October, and the town's famous Holiday Celebration. That just scratches the surface; for details on times and dates, as well as many other events, head to the city's website!

These festivals feature music, food, costumes, and a lot of fun and laughter. The town will be festooned with flowers or lights, the chicken dinners will be rolling off the stoves, and the key to success is participation. These are gatherings of celebrants, and you will be embraced as a friend, not a stranger, if you pay your ticket with a smile.

Bonding & Bridging

The community is a mix of old and new, but it has concentrated its Bavarian heritage in a small downtown area where horse-drawn carts and Bavarian architecture offset the busy street traffic.

You can use this time to acquaint your grandchildren with the classic tales of Heidi and the story of William Tell, and explore the wider German-speaking culture of Germany, Austria, and Switzerland. The Bavarian Belle Riverboat ride on the Cass River is a good place to share and reflect, or you can enjoy the horseback rides and Grandpa Tiny's Farm. If you are like us and want something even more remote and quiet, there are canoe rentals for the Cass River in nearby Vassar. If the festivities wear you out but your grandchildren need to play, there is an excellent children's museum in Saginaw.

A WORD TO THE WISE:

In addition to the large celebrations, the community offers many smaller experiences. If big crowds and lots of noise put you off, check out events like the Bavarian Inn pretzel rolling, the appearance of the Saginaw symphony, the Dixie Motor Speedways' Saturday night races, and the Farmers Market Earth Day celebration. Each event is fun and many are based on significant social causes.

AGE OF GRANDCHILD: 3 and up

CONTACT: Frankenmuth Chamber of Commerce and Convention & Visitors Bureau; 635 S Main St., Frankenmuth, MI 48734; (800) 386-8696; www.frankenmuth.org/festivals-and-events/festivals/

ALSO CHECK OUT:

African World Festival, Detroit: www.thewright.org/african-world-festival

Blue Water SandFest, Port Huron: www.bluewatersandfest.com

Holland Tulip Time Festival: www.tuliptime.com

Parade of Nations and International Ethnic Food Festival at Michigan Tech, Houghton: www.mtu.edu/international/events-programs/parade-nations/

Scottish Heritage, Alma: www.almahighlandfestival.com

I've learned that when your newly born grandchild holds your little finger in his fist, that you're hooked for life. ANDY ROONEY

Marshall M. Fredericks Sculpture Garden & Museum

Art adds to our love of life, our sense of self, and our perspective of the world. It reaches into our senses and touches us in special and unpredictable ways. But for our grandchildren, art can be difficult to relate to until they become accustomed to new points of view and perspectives. Sculpture is different. It is three-dimensional and therefore seems to be real.

Sculpture can be cartoonish, realistic, or even futuristic. It is something that our grandchildren relate to more easily than many other art forms. Michigan has wonderful sculptures in the parks and art galleries, but nothing compares

to the Marshall M. Fredericks Sculpture Garden & Museum at Saginaw Valley State University, just north of Saginaw. Here the artist's personality and creativity are on display both inside and outside.

Marshall Fredericks (1908–1998) could be called "Michigan's Sculptor." His work is found throughout Michigan and is particularly prominent in Detroit, in the zoo, and at the Frederik Meijer Gardens & Sculpture Park. His work is also well-known internationally. His sculptures are whimsical, comedic, happy, and easy to interpret. His credo begins with "I love people" and then he adds, "I want more than anything in the world to do sculpture that has real meaning for people . . . " Luckily, Saginaw Valley became the recipient of the Marshall work, because larger and more prestigious institutions did not move when Marshall's work became available.

The Marshall collection shares the insights and art of an individual who wrote, "I think any artist who forgets nature is losing a great deal of his life. Nature is so full, so manifold." Your grandchildren will see this in the way that he combines natural and human influences. He integrates nature, as do the natural areas and parks where they are often exhibited, places where people find their own happiness in a natural setting.

In addition, the exhibit includes the Sculptor's Studio, which helps you to understand the work that goes into giant sculptures like the *Spirit of Detroit*, which illuminates the city. From a small concept to a massive structure, each step is a work of art, but we seldom see what happens as the artist moves forward. It is a wonderful addition to sculpture.

Bonding & Bridging

We consider Marshall M. Frederick to be Michigan's unofficial state sculptor, and this presents a wonderful theme for exploring some of Michigan's best sites in a large-scale scavenger hunt! You could incorporate this idea into many travels, not just one trip, and it could be a wonderful theme for your voyages. We have found his sculptures in 41 Michigan communities! When you are looking for one sculptor's work, you will automatically discover the variations and excitement of other artists.

A WORD TO THE WISE:

Art often appeals to people with artistic talents, but for those who are less artistically inclined, the Sculpture Museum is ready to help. It offers a variety of programs throughout the year including art camps; the ones you must take advantage of are called "Second Saturdays," and they are specifically for grandparents and grandchildren. These include a guided tour, which is fun, but more importantly, they help you engage in the creative process of some sort; this might include drawing or sculpting and is based on examples in the museum. Think of how much fun you will have making your own art!

Places to look for Marshall Fredericks' sculptures include: the University of Michigan campus, Ann Arbor • Frederik Meijer Gardens & Sculpture Park, Grand Rapids • Cranbrook Campus, Bloomfield Hills • Detroit Zoo, Detroit • Municipal Center, Detroit • Interlochen Center for the Arts, Interlochen

AGE OF GRANDCHILD: 4 and up

BEST SEASON: All. Because the Marshall M. Fredericks Main Exhibit Gallery is on a college campus, it is easiest to visit on weekends and other off-days.

CONTACT: Marshall M. Fredericks Sculpture Garden & Museum, 7400 Bay Rd., University Center, MI 48710; (989) 964-7125; www.marshallfredericks.com

ALSO CHECK OUT:

Detroit Institute of Arts: www.dia.org

Frederik Meijer Gardens & Sculpture Park: www.meijergardens.org

Grand Rapids Art Museum: www.artmuseumgr.org

If I had known how wonderful it would be to have grandchildren, I'd have had them first. Lois Wyse

Hartwick Pines State Park and Logging Museum

An elevated boardwalk brings you to the Visitor Center at one of Michigan's largest state parks. Here a variety of exhibits focus on the history of logging, forestry, the ecology of our forests, and the use of trees in our daily lives. Large windows on all sides look out into the forest.

The giant trees stand in testament to the great white pine forests that once blanketed most of the Great Lakes region and covered an estimated 10 million acres. The land itself was shaped by glacial deposits into rolling hills, which over time grew into the forests that supplied the materials needed for develop-

ment of much of the young United States' towns and cities. Today there are 49 acres of white pines left, and they are between 250 and 400 years old—the only such stand found in the Lower Peninsula. To walk among these trees is to walk through a living historical museum. You have to crane your neck far back to see the tops, which reach over 150 feet into the air. The trail is asphalt, and visitors are asked to stay on it, since the roots of the trees are very shallow and if the soil becomes compacted from too many feet, it can injure the trees and even kill them over time. Some of these giants have fallen, their roots hanging in the air.

The Old Growth Trail is a mile and a quarter long. You can take your own tour, following along with a brochure. Or, you can go for a one-hour tour led by a park naturalist who will discuss the area's history and talk about the trees, the wildlife, and the many birds you will hear singing around you.

The trail reaches the Logging Museum area built in the 1930s by the Civilian Conservation Corps. Mrs. Karen Hartwick donated 8,000 acres of land to the state to create a state park. Her father had been one of the principal owners of a logging company that harvested much of the surrounding forest. In addition to the impact on the economy and life of the area, the replica of a logging camp allows future generations to see what life was like for the men who permanently changed the landscape and who believed that the supply of trees would never end.

Bonding & Bridging

Walking hand in hand with a grandchild through an old-growth forest has a great deal of symbolism. Like little saplings, they stand in your shadow ready to reach for the great heights you represent. But even as old as we may seem to the young ones, these trees are the oldest living things we may ever encounter. Talk about the importance of forests and how necessary they are in our lives—how they were necessary to make the paper for this book. Reflect on the years it takes to create wood and the speed with which we can consume it. It is important to know that we can also plant and grow forests for the future. Tell your grandchildren what you would like to see preserved for the future, so that someday they can enjoy the same pleasures with their grandchildren.

A WORD TO THE WISE:

There are special events at the park throughout the summer season that your grandchildren will enjoy; they include Wood Shaving Days with its emphasis on woodcraft, Iron Crafting Days, which celebrates blacksmithing skills, and Forest Fest, where Smokey Bear makes an occasional appearance. Activities at the Logging Museum include a steam-powered sawmill, as well as demonstrations by artisans and craftspeople. On weekends in the winter you can visit the center to ski or check out snowshoes!

AGE OF GRANDCHILD: Toddler to teenager

BEST SEASON: Summer

CONTACT: 4216 Ranger Rd., Grayling, MI 49738; (989) 348-2537
  • www.michigan.gov/hartwickpinesvc

ALSO CHECK OUT:

Porcupine Mountains Wilderness State Park:
www.michigandnr.com/parksandtrails/Details.aspx?type=SPRK&id=426

Tahquamenon Falls State Park:
www.michigandnr.com/parksandtrails/Details.aspx?type=SPRK&id=428

A baby is God's opinion that the world should go on. CARL SANDBURG

19

Interlochen Center for the Arts

Are you musical? Do you see musical talent in your grandchildren? Or are you like me and wish you could have been blessed with more talent than just being able to turn on the CD player? There is no place we have visited that makes music more vital, more exciting, and more kid-friendly than Interlochen.

We were drawn by its public radio station. It's a wonderful resource that entertained us as we drove, but more than that, it engaged us in the musical world,

which we found when we visited the summer campus of this great facility. Here, children play music enjoy amid nature in an open campus that invites visitors to concerts and special days.

Grandparents and grandchildren can share the beauty of music by walking the campus and stepping in to see and hear students playing everything from classical to jazz. Many famous performers come to the campus for concerts, but it is not the famous who are really important here—it's the students committed to music. Your grandchildren will be amazed by the sight of so many young people obviously having a good time while improving their musical abilities.

Come on a nice summer day and stop at the Visitor Center to get a schedule of the day's events and performances. They will tell you if there are places you can't visit. Then walk through the tree-lined campus and let the music filter out of the buildings and into you.

Finish your walk by choosing one of the student presentations. Sometimes it is a very important recital and you can feel the pressure in the room. At other times students are practicing or experimenting and the mood is light and creative.

Bonding & Bridging

Music is a universal way to communicate. What tribe, nation, or culture does not have music in its history or identity? Each generation takes the pulse of the culture and tries to create its own rhythmic statement. Over the decades we have gone from native percussion to minstrels to classics to gospel to folk to country to jazz to big band to blues to rock to heavy metal to hip-hop and rap, and each language has been created to separate the generations. But music is universal, and ultimately if we are exposed to enough variations, we can find beauty in many forms. That is what you can explore. Who did you like and why? What did the music express? What were the themes? In music you might find you really do have a lot in common.

A WORD TO THE WISE:

Check the website if you want to coordinate your visit with a special performance. There are over 600 events every year, so chances are good that you can find a time and performance to coincide with your visit. You can combine the concert with a campus tour in June, July, or August. The tours are much more than a walk-through. You can visit classes and sit in on rehearsals. It is a true backstage experience that will give your grandchildren additional insights and inspiration.

AGE OF GRANDCHILD: 7 and up

BEST SEASON: Summer

CONTACT: Interlochen Center for the Arts, 4000 Highway M-137, Interlochen, MI 49643; (231) 276-7200; www.interlochen.org

ALSO CHECK OUT:

Ann Arbor Folk Festival:
www.theark.org/shows-events/events-workshops/folk-festival

Gilmore International Keyboard Festival in Kalamazoo:
www.gilmore.org/plan-your-visit

Hiawatha Music Festival, Marquette: www.hiawathamusic.org

Ann Arbor Summer Festival: www.a2sf.org

*Joy in looking and comprehending is
nature's most beautiful gift.* ALBERT EINSTEIN

20

Tall Ship Sailing

"Swab the deck!" "Walk the plank!" "Shiver me timbers, Matey!" If these phrases sound old-fashioned, think again. A recent resurgence in all things pirate will have your grandchild jumping with excitement at the chance to actually board and sail away on a tall ship. No matter that the ship has electronic navigation equipment, a diesel engine, and lifeboats; it will still look like a pirate's bark in your grandchild's eyes.

In order to qualify as a schooner, a ship has to have two or more masts, with the forward mast being shorter or the same height as the rear masts. Cargo schooners have a long and significant place in the history of the Great Lakes. As early as 1679, explorers built ships with tall masts to sail across the lakes in search of their own form of treasure—natural resources—from the unsettled

wilderness. At one time there were more than 2,000 of these big-masted ships serving as cargo carriers. But over the course of their history, they've also served as warships, fishing boats, and pleasure craft on the Great Lakes.

In the 1980s and '90s there was a resurgence of sailing ships as passenger cruisers, but there are now just a handful. In Traverse City, you can board the tall ship *Manitou* daily during the summer season and sail for two hours, enough time to move far away from shore, raise a sail, catch a breeze, and feel the ship rock and roll on the waves. While younger grandchildren will imagine themselves in a swashbuckler movie, older grandchildren will be given a chance to help hoist the sails and take the wheel. Some grandchildren will simply enjoy the sunbathing opportunities on deck with a constant breeze to cool them. Every day on the 3–5 p.m. sail, the ship serves two scoops of the famous Moomers Homemade Ice Cream. On Wednesday evenings in July and August, you can go for a sail and be entertained by a musical group that sings about the sailing life.

This is an adventure that can be the culmination of time spent together reading tales of famous pirates and other sailing adventurers. The *Hornblower* series (on CD, tape, or DVD) is one such collection that will create images of sailing the high seas. For the younger grandchildren, fitting them out with a three-cornered hat or a bandana, an eye patch, and a sash will make them feel even more a part of the setting. But it's also a good time to just talk about the energy we can capture from the wind. Look how it can move a 100-ton ship and how in the future it just may be used to power our homes and businesses. Think of how many ways the wind works for us in turning our big generators or supporting the flight of our kites. When the wind blows, we feel the air and know that it has substance. The weight of the air pushing things over and holding things up was enough to inspire scientists to create elaborate experiments to understand the invisible blanket that surrounds us and supports life.

A WORD TO THE WISE:

If it is a particularly windy, wavy day and you have a grandchild with a touchy stomach, you may want to postpone your trip. Getting seasick is not the sort of memory you want them to have. There are some non-prescription medicines you can take before you board, such as Dramamine, but they often have the unintended consequence of making the person so sleepy that they might snore through an entire trip. Also, if you have young children aboard you can ask for life jackets; make sure they wear them the whole time.

AGE OF GRANDCHILD: 4 to teenager

BEST SEASON: Summer

CONTACT: 13258 SW Bay Shore Dr., Traverse City, MI 49684; (231) 941-2000; www.tallshipsailing.com

ALSO CHECK OUT:

Appledore Tall Ships, Bay City: www.baysailbaycity.org

Inland Seas Education Association, Suttons Bay: www.schoolship.org

Superior Odyssey, Marquette: www.superiorodyssey.com

The charm of a woodland road lies not only in its beauty but in anticipation. Around each bend may be a discovery, an adventure. DALE REX COMAN

21

Sleeping Bear Dunes National Lakeshore

The early Ojibwa are credited with naming this unique geologic site. Their legend tells of a mother bear and her two cubs fleeing a forest fire to the west and plunging into Lake Michigan in an attempt to reach the far shore. The mother got across first and climbed a tall bluff to wait and watch for her cubs, but they sank beneath the waves, forming North and South Manitou Islands. Their mother still waits for them in the form of the massive sand dune. The Sleeping Bear is just one of the many dunes that make up the largest freshwater sand dune complex in North America.

It isn't often we humans get to witness geologic events, other than catastrophic ones like volcanoes or earthquakes. The slow evolution of landscapes takes many human lifetimes, except among sand dunes. These massive mounds of glacially deposited sands move every year due to the force of wind, water, and ice. The dunescape you walk with your grandchild is not the one you climbed as a child. Maybe there was a living forest, where now all that is left are just "ghost" trees with bare trunks protruding from the sand.

It's probably best to preface your dune climbing by a visit to the Philip A. Hart Visitor Center in Empire. Here you can get a quick, but comprehensive, overview of the park and its geologic and human history. The Dune Climb is the one location you must visit. Grandchildren, and let's admit it, even grand-

parents, consider these mountains of moving silica grains to be giant playgrounds. Here you can run, jump, roll, and dig to your heart's content. But confine your activities to areas without grasses or small sand cherry plants. These are the colonizers whose job is to stabilize the dune and slow its forward motion, and they're easily uprooted by human foot traffic.

There is much more to see and do here, too: scenic drives, historic sites, trails in forests, and slow, meandering streams, but they all will have a hard time competing with this natural playground. Be sure to let the kids know you will climb the hills more slowly than they will and they need to stay within view at all times. It's easy to get disoriented once you get over the top of the dune, as footpaths go off in different directions.

Dunes serve as a reminder of the "shifting sands of time" and reinforce the desire and effort to spend as much time with the grandchildren as possible. The kids will want you to watch them leap and roll, and if you are able to do either, join them. Laughter will erupt all around and there is nothing that sets memories in place as surely as laughter. Climb the 130 feet to the top of the dune and look in all directions, maybe even bring a picnic to share on the beach. Even when you reach the top of the dune, the lake is still a long ways away and would require much more hill climbing, so you probably don't want to promise a swimming break. Do bring sand pails and shovels and trucks for the little ones and a Frisbee for the older kids. This is a great place for the kids to wear themselves out while you sit on the soft sand, watching and applauding their acrobatics.

A WORD TO THE WISE:

Be sure to wear shoes. The sand is hot in the summer sun, plus you never know who might have carelessly dropped garbage that can cause injury. Avoid the base of the dunes, and don't bury anyone (like you would on a beach) because landslides sometimes occur. Be sure to bring plenty of water and sunscreen. There is a drinking fountain near the parking lot but little shade. An early morning or late afternoon visit is probably the most enjoyable and will be the least crowded.

AGE OF GRANDCHILD: Toddler to teenager

BEST SEASON: Summer

CONTACT: Philip A. Hart Visitor Center: On Highway M-72, 500 feet east of M-22 in Empire; (231) 326-4700, ext. 5010

Dune Climb: From Empire, take M-22 north for 2 miles to M-109, then left on M-109 for 4 miles; www.nps.gov/slbe/index.htm

ALSO CHECK OUT:

Pictured Rocks National Lakeshore: www.nps.gov/piro

Warren Dunes State Park:
www.michigandnr.com/parksandtrails/Details.aspx?type=SPRK&id=504

Elephants and grandchildren never forget. ANDY ROONEY

22

Oden State Fish Hatchery

Michigan's abundant lakes, streams, and rivers are an angler's dream. As soon as people wandered into this region, they discovered the vast resources of the finned food found in the water. There are over 25,000 miles of coolwater streams and 11,000 miles of coldwater streams, and each type supports diverse fish communities.

As the human population grew with the arrival of the European settlers, development boomed around the Great Lakes, leading to massive habitat change, dam construction, pollution, and unregulated, unsustainable fishing. By the late 1800s, the fish populations were crashing and the state stepped in to try to reverse this desperate situation. In 1901, the Harrietta State Fish Hatchery opened. Others followed in the next two decades. By this time, alien species of fish had been added to the list of problems, with sea lampreys and alewives entering the system through the canals built between the Great Lakes. Hatchery-raised fish in Michigan today make up 40 percent of all recreational fishing catches.

Today at each of the state fisheries, you can take guided tours to see the work involved in raising millions of fish each year for release into Michigan streams. The Oden Fish Hatchery has a couple of especially interesting exhibits. One is a stream-viewing chamber, built directly beneath an actual stream, with windows on either side that let you look into the world inhabited by brown trout, rainbow trout and brook trout. This stream feeds into a pond where lunkers swim close to the surface, waiting for someone to throw a handful of food to them. There are dispensing stations around the pond that will eat your coins as quickly as your grandchild can throw the food into the pond. Everyone will enjoy seeing the water swirl and the dark bodies rise to the surface. This will probably be your grandchild's favorite spot. Come prepared with coins in your pocket.

There is also a historic train car parked in front of the Visitor Center that has been renovated and equipped with displays and a sound system to replicate the appearance and sounds heard from 1914 to 1935 aboard one of the "fish cars." These were used to transport fish from one location to another. From the train car to the pond it is a one-mile loop, and this is part of the self-guided nature trails on the property.

Bonding & Bridging

You likely have fond memories of lazy summer days spent by a pond or stream with a fishing pole pointed over the water and a red-and-white bobber marking the spot where that record-breaking sunny was sure to be waiting. Fishing, in many ways, is the antithesis of recreation for many children today. Where's the action? Fishing teaches one a lot about patience and finding pleasure in the unknown. Even if you never were much for fishing yourself, it is a lifelong hobby you should at least introduce your grandchild to, and a fish hatchery and stock pond is a good place to start, because you have all the educational exhibits and displays, not to mention a knowledgeable tour guide who can teach you and your grandchild the ways of fish—their habitat needs, preferred foods, and general biology—all good things for the successful angler to know.

A WORD TO THE WISE:

While you can always put together a private fishing expedition for your grandchild and yourself, the Oden Fish Hatchery has some special events on Tuesdays in July, known as "Brown Trout Tuesdays." These are free events that require pre-registration after Memorial Day. All equipment is provided, and a park interpreter will help explain proper fishing technique. You can watch as your grandchild spends half an hour trying to catch one of those great big trout swimming about in the big fish pond. Participation is limited to 12 children per half hour.

AGE OF GRANDCHILD: 4 to teenager

BEST SEASON: Summer

CONTACT: Oden Fish Hatchery, 3377 US-31, Oden, MI 49864; (231) 348-0998; www.michigan.gov/odenvc

ALSO CHECK OUT:

Platte River State Fish Hatchery, Beulah:
www.michigan.gov/dnr/0,1607,7-153-10364_28277-22491--,00.html

Thompson State Fish Hatchery, Manistique:
www.michigan.gov/dnr/0,1607,7-153-10364_28277-22486--,00.html

Wolf Lake State Fish Hatchery Visitor Center, Mattawan:
www.michigan.gov/dnr/0,4570,7-153-10364_52259_28277-22498--,00.html

The fire is the main comfort of the camp, whether in summer or winter, and is about as ample at one season as at another. It is as well for cheerfulness as for warmth and dryness. HENRY DAVID THOREAU

23

Mackinac Island

Back in 1898, the introduction of cars on Mackinac (pronounced "mak-i-naw") Island scared the horses and disturbed the peace so much that they were permanently banned on the island. That alone will impress your grandkids when they visit the island with you. Travel is by foot, bike, or horse-drawn carriage. It is a wondrous return to a nearly forgotten time.

Some 490 people live on the island year-round, many descendants of the Anishinaabe people who originally occupied this hump of limestone between Lake Michigan and Lake Huron. Their name for the island was "Michilimackinac," which meant "land of the large turtle." In the late 1600s, the Europeans landed and Father Marquette set up a mission for his Huron followers; then in the late 1700s, the British moved from the fortification across the strait to the island to give themselves a better defensive position

against the upstart American revolutionaries. After the end of the Revolution and the end of the War of 1812, island owner-ship bounced between the British and Americans, but finally the Americans took possession and invited traders to set up shop. First the economy was centered on the American Fur Company, then commercial fishing, and finally after the Civil War, tourism.

In 1875, Mackinac Island became the country's second national park, and later became a state park in 1895. Hotels sprang up, including the Grand Hotel, which still shines like a beacon. Things slowed down between the Great Depression and World War II, but after that conflict ended, tourism resumed and hasn't slowed since. In fact, the Park Commission is trying to buy more land to protect and preserve the unique qualities of the quiet, early twentieth-century lifestyle.

Even though the island is only 2,200 acres, there are so many things to do that it requires an extended stay or multiple visits. The Historic Fort at the top of the hill is well preserved, as are the commercial and residential buildings on Market Street. Tours of both include reenactors dressed in period clothing, ready to share their knowledge. You won't be able to avoid the sweet shops. This industry sprang up in 1889, and by the 1920s Mackinac was synonymous with fudge. In June, there is a Lilac Festival with one of the largest parades in Michigan—the only one where all the floats are pulled by horses.

According to the old saying, you never forget how to ride a bike. That's probably true, but sometimes our sense of balance or our legs don't continue to function as they once did. However, if you are still able to ride a bike, this is the place to do it. There is a paved path that goes all the way around—8 miles. It is 90 percent flat, so neither you nor the kids will have trouble with hills. There are picnic tables scattered along the way and some rocky beaches to explore. You may have to slalom around horse apples, but the kids will probably consider that a bonus challenge. You can bring your own bikes over on the ferry or rent one of the thousands that are on the island, including tandems and tagalongs for younger kids who are learning to ride and are too big for the rickshaw-like trailers. Let the kids know you are riding on Lake Shore Boulevard, also known as "M-185," the only Michigan state highway that doesn't allow cars. You don't have to make the entire circuit either—you can always go part way and turn back. The important thing is to enjoy the ride.

A WORD TO THE WISE:

Because it is an island, food prices are high. You can reduce your expenses by packing a picnic lunch (if you're there for just the day) or bring a cooler with some sandwich makings and beverages in it, for a longer stay. Also, bring along a Frisbee, baseball glove and ball, or possibly a kite. There are large open fields in front of the Historic Fort and on the waterfront perfect for these old-fashioned pursuits. Try to get the kids to leave the electronic toys behind—on an island where cars are banned, so, too, should be toys that beep and blink. Also be aware that weekends, holidays, and festivals are the busiest times. The streets can be so crowded that it feels like a state fair or maybe Mardi Gras in New Orleans. Keep a sharp eye out for distracted bike riders.

AGE OF GRANDCHILD: 4 and up

BEST SEASON: Summer

CONTACT: Mackinac Island Tourism Bureau, 7274 Main St., Mackinac Island, MI 49757; (906) 847-3783; www.mackinacisland.org

ALSO CHECK OUT:

Beaver Island: www.beaverisland.org

Drummond Island: www.drummondislandchamber.com

Isle Royale: www.nps.gov/isro

It is not a slight thing when they who are so fresh from God, love us. **Charles Dickens**

24

Historic Mill Creek Discovery Park

You may have visited Historic Mill Creek—it's a beautifully forested 625-acre preserve designed to show visitors how the early settlers of the area turned the surrounding forests into lumber and built the community on Mackinac Island. But if you look at the name again, you will see the addition of two important words—Discovery Park. This state historic site is adding some exciting and fun elements to an already excellent historic educational program. The Forest Canopy Bridge and Eagle's Flight Zip Line are two components of the Adventure Tour. There is nothing that excites kids more than the somewhat scary challenge of walking high aboveground (in this case 50 feet)

and then "flying" through the air for 425 feet from the treetops to ground level. The third component of the Adventure Tour is a 40-foot-high Nature Trail climbing wall.

The fourth component of the Adventure Tour is the park naturalist who leads each small group and provides an interpretive talk about the plants and wildlife found in this northern forest biome from a perspective few people ever get. For those who prefer to stay on ground level, there is the fascinating water-powered sawmill and a sawpit demonstration, where young members of the audience are recruited to help demonstrate the two-person sawing technique of old. There are other reconstructed buildings to wander through, but if you have young children you will want to visit the new additions.

The Water Power Station is a fun way for young and old alike to experience a real watermill. Just playing with the water provides endless fun, but there will be lessons gained, all nearby the actual sawmill. The Forest Friends Play area, with its climbable fiberglass animals and imprinted animal tracks, is another place for the little ones to play while Grandma and Grandpa take a break and act as spectators.

This historic site also includes five trails of varying lengths and difficulty. and gives you and the kids a chance to burn off some energy and enjoy the beauty of stream, forest, and bluffs. With the new additions to this site, expect your grandchildren to ask, "Can we come here again?" at the end of each visit.

Bonding & Bridging ✕✕✕✕✕✕✕✕✕✕✕✕✕✕✕✕✕✕✕✕✕✕✕✕✕✕✕

At first glance, the grandkids may think you're just taking them to another historical place, but when they see the elevated walkway and zip line they will change their attitude—especially when they know that you are going to go with them on this adventure. Life is full of challenges, and putting ourselves outside our comfort zone once in a while is good for everyone. We expect youngsters to try new things, but what do they think about us old folks? That our days of adventure are over? Well, show the kids that we set those limits. Granted, you may have a physical condition that doesn't allow you to participate and your grandchildren will understand and accept that, but if you are physically able, then it's strictly mind over matter. Your grandchildren will forever remember and talk about the day Grandma went zipping down and over the creek, smiling all the way. And you can be their cheerleader as they clip in and zip away. This is a shared experience that combines adrenaline, nervous laughter, and maybe even sweaty palms, but oh, the exhilaration!

A WORD TO THE WISE:

The Adventure Tour isn't for everyone. It's good to encourage young and old to participate, but no one should be forced into it. And if after starting out on the tour, anyone feels really uncomfortable, they should be allowed to return without any sense of failure. This should be fun—not stressful. Each individual will wear a safety harness and be clipped into a cable overhead. You must weigh between 50 and 250 pounds and be at least four feet tall to participate. Safety instructions will be given before each tour, and it's your responsibility to make sure your child pays attention and obeys all the rules. Parents must sign a release form before children participate in the Adventure Tour.

AGE OF GRANDCHILD: 5 to teenager

BEST SEASON: Summer

CONTACT: 9001 US-23, Mackinaw City, MI 49701; (231) 436-4100 (Mackinac Island State Historic Parks); www.mightymac.org/millcreekpark.htm

ALSO CHECK OUT:

Colonial Michilimackinac, Mackinaw City:
www.mackinacparks.com/parks-and-attractions/colonial-michilimackinac/

Keweenaw National Historic Park, Houghton: www.nps.gov/kewe

*Sunshine is delicious, rain is refreshing, wind braces
us up, snow is exhilarating; there's really no such thing as
bad weather, only different kinds of good weather.* JOHN RUSKIN

25

Colonial Michilimackinac

Like most early settlements and forts built in the early 1700s, Michilimackinac was situated near water, in this case, the Straits of Mackinac. As strange as it may seem today, in 1715 this was considered the northwest frontier of the continent. The French constructed this stockade settlement, and some of the 13 reconstructed buildings inside are made in the French style with logs set upright in the ground and slabs of cedar bark overlapping on the roofs. As you enter the reconstructed fort through the Water Gate, you will see the fur-trading colonial village firsthand.

Colonial Michilimackinac is unique because of the archaeological work that continues today. It has lasted 50 years so far, making it the longest-running continuous archaeological dig in the U.S. It is now about 60 percent complete. This slow and tedious process ensures the reconstructed buildings and the information shared with visitors are as accurate as possible. You can observe the dig yourself and ask questions of the workers who carefully sift sand through wire mesh, searching for artifacts and remnants of life in the past. Two of the buildings in the complex incorporate parts of the dig, letting you peer down through plexiglass windows to see examples of pots and other items found. In the Chevalier House, you can walk down steps to enter a room enclosed by glass on three sides and see the charred timbers that once housed the powder magazine.

This fort has costumed reenactors who are always popular with kids, and throughout the day there are scheduled presentations that include musket and cannon firing, children's games of that era, and a French Colonial wedding and dance. Once per afternoon, a group of voyageurs, always a rowdy lot, arrives at the Water Gate. Some buildings have live demonstrators, while others have posed mannequins. One building has a small collection of items for the younger children to try on and pretend to be settlers or soldiers.

There is room to run here, and the elevated walkway that encircles the stockade may be the most fun for your grandkids. Here, they can look out and get a bird's-eye perspective of the settlement and imagine being a soldier looking out at the unsettled wilderness beyond the walls.

A fort like this must seem ancient to a child, and it is a good place to focus on what we keep and pass on to our descendants. An "old place" like this helps us consider what we value and what future generations may think about our lifestyles. Ask the kids if there is anything you own that they would like to pass on to their grandchildren, or tell them if there is something you have that you consider really special and want to pass on to them.

While the memories of the times we spend together will always be the most precious gifts we can pass along, there are certain material things that come to signify some aspect of our relationships. Maybe it is a hat you always wear, or a fishing rod you use, or a porcelain bowl you always use to make cookies. They don't need to be expensive to have value; they just need to have had your touch and care to make them special in the eyes of your grandchild.

A WORD TO THE WISE:

Before you can visit the historic fort, you enter the Visitor's Center. It has a large gift shop, but avoid that until you've seen the fort so you can choose a souvenir appropriate for your visit. There is an introductory film you should watch, even if your grandchild balks and asks to skip the movie. It is well done, only 13 minutes long, and gives you a good intro to what you'll see and hear inside the fort and fur-trading village.

AGE OF GRANDCHILD: 3 to 13

ADDRESS: 102 W Straits Ave., Mackinaw City, MI 49701

CONTACT: Located under the south approach to the Mackinac Bridge; (231) 436-4100 (Mackinac State Historic Parks); www.mackinacparks.com

ALSO CHECK OUT:

Historic Mill Creek Discovery Park: www.mackinacparks.com/parks-and-attractions/historic-mill-creek-discovery-park/

Keweenaw National Historic Park, Houghton: www.nps.gov/kewe/

Wisdom begins in wonder. SOCRATES

26

Museum of Ojibwa Culture

At this museum, which is a former church, you will have a chance to see and interact with exhibits and displays that describe the materials and beliefs that allowed the Ojibwa to live and prosper in this northern landscape. First of all, you will learn the name they call themselves is "Anishinaabeg," which

means "original" or "first man." They were called "Ojibwa" by their neighbors, and later that word was changed to "Chippewa" by the English-speaking travelers who came next. The original meaning of "Ojibwa" is thought to mean "those who made pictographs."

Many of us know very little about how American Indians lived except for the Hollywood interpretations, which are often inaccurate and stereotypical. What's more, most characterizations are based on the cultures of Plains Indians, which is far removed from the dense woodlands found in our region.

As you wander through the museum, you will see some of the tools these people used in their daily lives; you can show these to your grandchild and ask them if they think it would be difficult to make tools from stone, bone, or copper. Then look at the baskets and bowls and admire the intricate designs, some made with beads and others using porcupine quills. Walk through the store and show the grandkids the quill boxes, jewelry, and baskets crafted by contemporary American and Canadian indigenous peoples.

You can watch a short film about Ojibwa family life inside a replica of a birch Huron hut. Continue on and you will see a life-size diorama of a typical Ojibwa family camp. This has been updated with actual American Indian items and jewelry hand-painted by local native artists.

In the same section, you will find a new display depicting the government boarding schools that indigenous children were forced to attend, even recently. You can explain to your grandchildren how bad the indigenous children must have felt when they were taken away from their parents and were forced to stop speaking their native language, cut their hair, and wear European-style clothing.

All in all, this is the perfect place to introduce your children to the nuances—and costs—of history.

Ask your grandchildren what American Indians are like, and they may tell you they live in teepees, wear feathers in their hair and shoot arrows at people—the image that the entertainment industry has perpetuated for decades. A trip to the Museum of Ojibwa Culture is about more than introducing your grandchildren to another culture. It's about teaching them the negative aspects of stereotyping. They may assume that American Indians were (and perhaps still are) violent and scary. Talk with them about stereotypes and how they harm others. Would they like it if people judged them without getting to know them first? They are going to live in a world where they will encounter people from different cultures often. It will require an open mind and heart to recognize the similarities we share with others and the understanding that differences are often superficial. This conversation will help to create an awareness of other people and their feelings.

A WORD TO THE WISE:

The grounds around the museum are actually the areas where the Huron people once had their longhouses. There is a longhouse you can look at (but not walk through), and it's quite a sight. There is also a beautiful award-winning park along the side of the museum depicting the clan animals that each member of the tribes belonged to. Each clan had specific jobs to do in the daily life of the tribe.

While there you can also check out the medicine wheel garden behind the museum. It is the symbol of the beliefs of the Ojibwa and a symbol of the circle of life. Each of the four sections has its own sacred plant.

AGE OF GRANDCHILD: 3 to teenager

BEST SEASON: Summer

CONTACT: 500 N State St., St. Ignace, MI 49781; (906) 643-9161; www.museumofojibwaculture.net

ALSO CHECK OUT:

Nokomis Learning Center, Okemos: www.nokomis.org

Ziibiwing Center, Mount Pleasant: www.sagchip.org/ziibiwing/

Bringing up a family should be an adventure, not an anxious discipline in which everybody is constantly graded for performance. MILTON R. SAPERSTEIN

27

The Locks at Sault Ste. Marie

Located between two countries and connecting the two largest Great Lakes, the famous Soo Locks are both a fascinating engineering feat and a compromise with nature. The locks are located in a natural waterway—the St. Marys River—where the native populations fished the rapids in birchbark canoes. This was the waterway of famous French Canadian explorers, and it sits today across the Canadian and Michigan cities of the same name, Sault Ste. Marie, facing off like two ice hockey greats across the straits.

You can view the locks from the new American Visitor Center and climb into the bleachers to observe and cheer on massive ships that fill all but a few inches of the concrete containers. On the American side, the locks move the major ships; you can watch the doors open to let ships in or out as commerce moves from the Northland through the lakes, and sometimes out the St. Lawrence Seaway to the ocean.

Children will be closer to the big "Lakers" and "Salties" here than almost anywhere, and they'll get to see them actually engaged in commerce. They will see the large ships in these small temporary aquariums and observe how the water of Lake Superior flows into the locks, step by step, until the water is at the same level as Lake Superior when the ship is northbound, and how the water is let out of the locks to lower it to the level of the St. Marys River for southbound shipping.

Visit the museum, see the displays, see the boats, and then take a ride on a tour boat. There is nothing better than riding up to the massive structure and then traveling in. The doors close. There is a sense of anticipation and mystery, but the rise is steady and smooth and soon the tour boat will move into Lake Superior. Typically the boat tour will show you some of the local industry, and then return through the much smaller and historical Canadian Locks, and downstream again. As you enter the river from the Canadian Locks, you can enjoy the shoreline and statues of the Canadian city and then look off toward the states and see a portion of the famous rapids, still churning whitewater around the rocks.

Float downstream, keep turning around to see different views, and you'll reach the end of the ride with a much better appreciation of the area.

Bonding & Bridging

While other locations teach you about the shipwrecks and hazards of the open freshwater seas, this is a working landscape where you can help your grandchildren explore the industries and history of iron ore, the fur trade, and the international shipping that has influenced our country and the local communities.

Visit the large museum ship *Valley Camp,* and experience the size of the ship as you walk from one end to the other and climb up the various levels. Talk about what it must be like to cross these big lakes, especially in storms and in the late fall when the famous nor'easters blow and icicles hang from the rails. Then climb the Tower of History and get a view of all the places you explored. We have all experienced sea stories about pirates and explorers, but only a few of us really go to sea. Combine this ship with the trip through the locks and you will have shared great knowledge and memories.

A WORD TO THE WISE:

Your trip is not really complete unless you spend some time on the Canadian side. The small museum by the old lock is historic and adds new information. But it is the walk along the small locks that really helps you explore. This is a more intimate setting where the locks are less imposing and a little easier to comprehend. Walk out on the island and see the natural beauty, and then continue to follow the path as it goes along the waterfront.

AGE OF GRANDCHILD: 4 and up

BEST SEASON: Summer

CONTACT: Soo Locks Visitor Center, Osborn Blvd., Sault Ste. Marie, MI 49783; Boat schedule hotline: (906) 253-9290; www.lre.usace.army.mil/Missions/Recreation/Soo-Locks-Visitor-Center

Soo Locks Boat Tours, Dock #1, 1157 E Portage Ave., and Dock #2, 515 E Portage Ave., Sault Ste. Marie, MI 49783; (800) 432-6301, (906) 632-6301; www.soolocks.com

ALSO CHECK OUT:

Beaver Island Boat Company, Charlevoix: www.bibco.com/tours-6/

Museum Ship Valley Camp: www.saulthistoricsites.com

Shepler's Mackinac Island Ferry: www.sheplersferry.com

Books are the treasured wealth of the world and the fit inheritance of generations and nations. HENRY DAVID THOREAU

28

The Birds of Whitefish Point

Imagine how much energy a bird needs to fly hundreds of miles. Think of how much they must travel and where they might refuel. Some birds migrate with their prey (like kestrels, which follow migrating dragonflies). Some eat along the way, and some make the long, difficult passages on the reserves they have stored up—such birds have a very high miles-per-calorie efficiency.

Large birds need more energy and either require more food or a boost in efficiency, which often comes in the form of thermals, or rising currents of hot air released by organic matter. Large birds take advantage of these currents, but nature is not uniform and the flows of such updrafts are not continuous.

When a lake is in the path, everything changes. Lakes hold in heat, take a long time to heat up, and consequently create cold pockets where the air sinks!

Then there is Lake Superior—talk about a cold air sink—this is like a mountain for birds, and they cross it at their own peril. So the birds often hesitate when they get to the shore and move laterally (east to west), congregating where the crossing is shortest—like Whitefish Point, which provides a quick leap to the Canadian shore.

You can find birds here in all seasons. Visit the small Visitor Center bookstore during the day to learn about the latest sightings, which are written on a whiteboard, and the staff will share what they know (a lot). This is a research site and they have data from many years of banding, counting, and observing.

But don't confine your activity to a walk along the beach; join them for some adventures that your family will find nowhere else. Guided bird watching trips may be geared for older grandchildren and adults, but real birders in the family can start pretty young. Trips are open to the general public every weekend. In the evenings, watch for the "owl flight" as experts help you find the elusive hunters of the night. During migration, they have a program called "Nocturnal Raptors Up Close," featuring birds that are caught in banding nets with other birds you can see up close. The end of April brings the Spring Fling, with talks by prominent bird experts and birding field trips. This is considered one of the top 30 bird watching spots in the country!

Bonding & Bridging

Bird watching is essentially a form of non-lethal hunting. It is a challenge to know where to look, to see the field marks, to recognize birdsong, to get close enough, with the light behind you and not the bird, to get the bird in your binoculars, and to get the binoculars focused. Whew! But when the optics fill with color, when you can open the field guide and say—"that's it," you have a shared success and you are ready for the next challenge.

A WORD TO THE WISE:

Whitefish Point always has birds, but it is primarily known as a "migration hotspot." Coming in the summer is nice but not satisfying if you are looking for lots of birds. March through May, and September into November are good months, and you can plan for what you might see by checking with the Visitor Center, but, in general, this is the pattern:

Mid-March: eagles

Late March to early April: large hawks

Mid- to late April: smaller accipiters (hawks) followed by falcons

Mid- to late May: broad-winged hawks

Mid-April and May: waterfowl fly low over the lake to avoid the raptors; throughout these flights a variety of songbirds come through

Fall: the pattern reverses itself beginning in September

AGE OF GRANDCHILD: 5 and up

BEST SEASON: Spring and fall

CONTACT: Whitefish Point Bird Observatory, 16914 N Whitefish Point Rd., Paradise, MI 49768-9612; (906) 492-3596; www.wpbo.org

ALSO CHECK OUT:

CraneFest: www.cranefest.org

Kirtland's Warbler tours:
www.michiganaudubon.org/kirtlands-warbler-tours/

Mackinac Straits Raptor Watch: www.mackinacraptorwatch.org

Pointe Mouillee Birding Trips: www.michigan.gov/dnr/0,4570,7-153-10370_62146_62150-283172--,00.html

Grandparents are made in Heaven, born with the birth of their first grandchild. Gail Lumet Buckley

29

Tahquamenon Falls State Park

There are so many waterfalls in the Upper Peninsula that one guidebook focuses entirely on them. It is more than likely that a few hidden waterfalls didn't even make the list, but only a few waterfalls stand alone as icons of a region. Niagara, Minnehaha, Yosemite, Yellowstone, and Iguazu all fit that category, and Tahquamenon, which has a drop of nearly 50 feet and is more than 200 feet across, deserves that status for Michigan. In fact, this seemingly remote wilderness falls was significant enough to draw Longfellow's attention

when he wrote the "Song of Hiawatha." He included it in the book-length epic poem—"by the rushing Tahquamenaw Hiawatha built his canoe"—and if you time it right, you can enjoy the annual canoe race on the river!

Set in a beautiful mature forest protected by Michigan's second-largest state park, there is an easy trail that makes seeing the falls simple for even young children and grandparents with limited mobility. Trees are marked along the way, and there is an interpretive gazebo where naturalists might help you and your grandchildren explore nature and ideas, or you can read and enjoy displays on your own; this will add to your knowledge of the park and resources.

Do not expect to be alone. There are close to 500,000 visitors annually, but because of the setting and the staggering beauty of the place, you will seldom notice how many others are here watching and contemplating. You can find distant views that take in a large part of the canyon, or you can take the trail to the steps and platform that put you right on top of the falls.

In fact, there are two different waterfalls at the park. The "upper falls" are larger, but the "lower falls," four miles to the northeast, are beautiful in their own right. So visit the upper falls or stroll down to the lower falls. Or you can do both, which is the best choice.

Wild places like this offer special opportunities to get close to the land. The beauty of the river is a natural draw, but making it into something more requires that grandparents do more than hike. Try to take advantage of the naturalist sessions if you can, so that you harness their enthusiasm and knowledge. Participate rather than watch. Demonstrate that you care, and the children will care. Show them how to learn and they will emulate you.

We have seen the power of making a good example with our grandchildren and the thousands of students we've witnessed during our professional careers in education. We know that when we connect with students they look to see what we do and how we act, what we value, and what we expect. Grandparents are natural leaders and teachers—it comes with the title. If you value reading, they will read. If you show respect and care for nature, they will have respect and care. When we share what we know, it is a great experience; when we share our ethics, it is one of our strongest bonds.

A WORD TO THE WISE:

This root beer-colored water stands out from the lush blues of the big lake and is sure to pique your grandchildren's curiosity. You can tell them that the water is colored by tannin—a product of trees and tree roots that gives tree bark its dark color and is also used in tanning leather. It is fun to have a few tidbits of information to share, and it is easy to go to websites and get checklists of animals or plants that you can look up ahead of time. The kids will love to have their wise grandparents help them learn a few things (but choose just enough to intrigue and not enough to bore).

AGE OF GRANDCHILD: All

BEST SEASON: Spring and fall

CONTACT: 41382 W M-123, Paradise, MI 49768; (906) 492-3415; www.michigandnr.com/parksandtrails/Details.aspx?type=SPRK&id=428

ALSO CHECK OUT:

Black River Scenic Byway, Bessemer: https://scenicbyways.info/byway/10780.html

Pictured Rocks National Lakeshore waterfalls: www.nps.gov/piro/planyourvisit/waterfalls.htm

Some family trees bear an enormous crop of nuts. Wayne Huizenga

30

Great Lakes Shipwreck Museum

Michigan borders four Great Lakes and has 11,000 inland lakes; that's an amazing amount of coastline. Michigan boasts over 100 lighthouses, the only Great Lakes underwater national park—Thunder Bay National Marine Sanctuary—the largest Great Lake dunes, and a coastline that rivals any ocean state. So what could capture this coastal spirit and its stories better than a museum that focuses on shipwrecks, lighthouses, and the life of a lighthouse keeper?

This museum is a walk through history and a perspective on the present. Right next to the Whitefish Point Bird Observatory and near Tahquamenon Falls, this location combines with its neighbors to give you a real North Country education. Start in the museum and your grandchildren will know why lighthouses are needed.

There are life-size diving suits and mannequins to help children understand what diving is like in the cold, clear lake full of wrecks from all eras. The

excellent models of these ships are on a scale that kids see in their own toys and make the story of the shipwrecks and sea adventures seem more real. The multimedia, 3-D displays help immerse you in the experience.

Outside, the discovery continues as you visit the oldest active light on Lake Superior and the keeper's quarters, constructed under orders from President Abraham Lincoln. The lifeboat station was established in 1923 and creates a good visual for understanding the unselfish heroism of men who would jump in these boats in the midst of roiling seas and at great risk to themselves, in an attempt to help others.

At the end of the boardwalk, you can stand under the lighthouse tower and look out at the magnificent beach and lake. From here you can look toward Canada and toward the locks. Just 17 miles from this point, the *Edmund Fitzgerald* went down in 1975, one of the most recent and dramatic shipwreck stories in the museum. The ship's bell is in the gallery and welcomes you to this place of honor.

Bonding & Bridging

While the stories are vivid and stir the imagination, they also emphasize the negative. A ship lost at sea, in a storm, is a nightmarish event, and one of great terror. These are the predominant images that the children will remember, and while these are captivating, they also require perspective. For every vessel that went down, there are thousands of ships around the world without problems. It is important that they understand the safety mechanisms in place, like lighthouses, firefighters, the Coast Guard, and the police, and they should know we take precautions. The water should be enjoyed, not feared; we used boats long before wheels. Let them see that shipwrecks are unusual events, and they will enjoy the water and you can have a partner for many great experiences on the water.

A WORD TO THE WISE:

A good way to balance this experience is to visit the neighboring Whitefish Point Bird Observatory where you can dwell on the beautiful and living. You can also add to the trip with a quiet visit to Point Iroquois Lighthouse, located on Lakeshore Drive at Bay Mills. This beautiful spot has a beach and a boardwalk and is on the way from Sault Ste. Marie to Whitefish Point. This is a different style of lighthouse and keeper's home and a nice addition to the experience.

AGE OF GRANDCHILD: 3 and up

BEST SEASON: Summer

CONTACT: 18335 N Whitefish Point Rd., Paradise, MI 49768; (888) 492-3747; www.shipwreckmuseum.com

ALSO CHECK OUT:

Dossin Great Lakes Museum: www.detroithistorical.org/main/dossin/index.aspx

Michigan Underwater Preserves: www.michiganpreserves.org

Straits of Mackinac Shipwreck Museum: www.mackinacparks.com/parks-and-attractions/old-mackinac-point-lighthouse/

Thunder Bay National Marine Sanctuary: thunderbay.noaa.gov/designation/history.html

The simplest toy, one which even the youngest child can operate, is called a grandparent. SAM LEVENSON

31

Seney National Wildlife Refuge

This is a place where people and nature come together to celebrate the rich diversity of life and the historic landscape that greeted our American Indian and pioneer ancestors. This refuge is a complex of wetlands and forest that is known locally as the Great Manistique Swamp, and it seems to be as pristine as any part of the Upper Peninsula. But that is another of the intriguing aspects of this magic land. In fact, this landscape was logged very heavily for its pines, hardwoods, and the contents of its "swamp" forests. This logging was followed by fires deliberately set to remove debris, and these fires had a negative impact on the soils and seedlings. If that weren't enough, a land company built ditches to drain the wetlands. Yet the area was so rich and important that in 1935, the U.S. Fish & Wildlife Service still saw its importance as wildlife

habitat. Some grandparents can relate to the disappearance of our resources, but grandchildren must be connected with nature through experience and observation.

The bogs and lakes make for a unique wilderness area with both hardwoods and conifers, which provide habitat for ducks, eagles, osprey, loons, swans, otters, beavers, bears, wolves, and an occasional moose. The place to start is the Visitor Center, where displays can help you learn what to look for. The inside displays have many mounted animals, and tell the story of the refuge and its importance. But to really see this story connect with your experience, just step outside and begin your observations here and familiarize yourself with the wetland that surrounds the building.

The seven-mile marshland drive through the heart of the refuge is perfect for walking, biking, and driving. This narrow roadway puts you very close to wildlife and wild lands and is a one-way street. In the spring and fall it passes through trees full of birds, but most of your attention will probably be drawn to the open water and the large swans, herons, geese, ducks, and loons. They are easy to see and identify, and it's intriguing to watch them and observe their behavior. You can also walk trails like the Pine Ridge Nature Trail near the Visitor Center. This trail is only 1.2 miles long, but it gives you a close look at many habitats, songbirds, and animal tracks. Other options include canoeing on the Manistique River, cross-country skiing, hunting, and fishing.

Bonding & Bridging

Wildlife refuges reflect our human desire to have a positive relationship with the other species that share our Earth. The effort to save species and yet to enjoy their presence is part of the experience at Seney. They are working to restore the landscape to near-original conditions where appropriate. Nonetheless, there is a large ditch onsite, and the pools that people drive around in the eastern portion of the refuge would not have been there before the refuge was established. The Civilian Conservation Corps created those pools in the 1930s and 1940s by installing a series of dikes and water control structures. The goal was to attract ducks, geese, and other waterfowl to the refuge for breeding purposes, but that didn't work as well as they had hoped. Today those pools are home to common loons, trumpeter swans, and ospreys—all state-threatened species; they also provide a nice habitat for many other waterbirds.

On the rest of the refuge, where appropriate, restoration is underway. In the wilderness area, Seney strives to preserve the habitats that are already close to the original conditions of the refuge.

A WORD TO THE WISE:

If you want to have a more intense visit you can take advantage of 50 miles of bike trails! But if you want a real bonding experience, take advantage of the blueberry picking allowed in the refuge. My grandmother would take me blackberry picking every summer and then we would come home and have blackberry pies. To say that made a strong impression would be an understatement. There is nothing like berry picking to expose your grandchildren to a slower pace, contact with nature, and share a wonderful memory.

AGE OF GRANDCHILD: 8 and up

BEST SEASON: The Refuge Visitor Center and Marshland Wildlife Drive are open from May 15 to October 20.

CONTACT: 1674 Refuge Entrance Rd., Seney, MI 49883; (906) 586-9851; www.fws.gov/refuge/seney

ALSO CHECK OUT:

Viewing Michigan Wildlife:
www.michigan.gov/dnr/0,4570,7-153-10370_12144---,00.html

Whitefish Point Bird Observatory: www.wpbo.org

If you don't know [your family's] history, then you don't know anything. You are a leaf that doesn't know it is part of a tree. MICHAEL CRICHTON

32

Fayette Historic State Park

Here, 19 historic buildings stand silently on the shore of a beautiful bay of northern Lake Michigan. The peninsula of land arches around a protected lagoon of still, clear water with a steep limestone cliff farther inland and poles where docks once stood. This is the perfect landscape for photography and watercolor painting, a place where you can let your little ones make art with a

small camera, by drawing pictures, or by making rubbings (placing paper over old boards and recording the textures by rubbing the paper with the side of a crayon). All of these steps help you record the fingerprints of history.

As quiet as it is now, from 1867 to 1891 the blast furnaces that once operated here produced 229,288 tons of iron and converted the limestone and forest into heat for the Jackson Iron Company. With the cost of transportation high, the mine owners smelted "pig iron" nearby, right by the harbor.

Fayette Brown was a company agent and the man who chose the site that would be one of the U.P.'s most productive smelting operations. With nearly 500 residents to work the furnaces and the charcoal kilns, this was an active town full of Canadians, Britons, and northern Europeans.

If you start in the Visitor Center, you can find a model of the town and read some stories from the community, and then take the trail down to the town site. The old buildings might not contain ghosts, but they do have wonderful displays of materials from the life of the miners and their families. Kids will enjoy seeing the things that filled the lives of the youngsters who lived in the soot and heat of the industry, a condition that was far from today's seemingly pristine environment. There are many buildings to visit, each with a different story and a trail that connects you to the lake and surroundings.

If you choose the second Saturday of August—Fayette's Heritage Day—you might even convince yourself that the ghosts have come alive while you enjoy the period costumes, food, music, and displays.

Bonding & Bridging

What do we mean when we call a place a "ghost town"? Does this image conjure frightening ghouls and danger? Or do you picture a place frozen in time, images that have managed to survive time and natural forces? If you are like us, we have scrapbooks and photo books that help us relive the past and bring back memories. Are these ghost books?

Our heritage and the history of our family, our country, and the world are fascinating and filled with both stories and lessons. Help your grandchildren understand they can look back through time and understand these stories, and explain that they, too, are making tracks in time that will be stories for future generations.

A WORD TO THE WISE:

If history is not your forte, or at least the history of this community isn't, take advantage of the 25-minute guided tour of the great limestone furnaces and beehive kilns as you explore the industry of this high-grade charcoal pig-iron operation. It's hard to imagine, but this pristine place was once so sooty, so muddy, hot, smoky, and dirty that it was compared to the worst slums of Cleveland, and in those days Cleveland's industrial landscape was not something you would want to experience. In fact, hanging the clothes out on a line got them dirty instead of dry!

AGE OF GRANDCHILD: 7 and older

BEST SEASON: Summer

CONTACT: 4785 II Rd., Garden, MI 49835; (906) 644-2603; www.michigandnr.com/parksandtrails/Details.aspx?type=SPRK&id=417

ALSO CHECK OUT:

Michigan Ghost Towns: www.ghosttowns.com/states/mi/mi.html

Port Crescent State Park: www.michigandnr.com/parksandtrails/Details.aspx?id=486&type=SPRK

Grandchildren are God's way of compensating us for growing old. MARY H. WALDRIP

33

Pictured Rocks National Lakeshore

What do you expect to see when you visit a lakeshore? A beach, umbrellas, bathers, the glisten of tanning oil, and a lot of energy and confusion? If so, this may not be the place for you. But if you want to have tranquility, watch the waves lap against multicolored rocks, find evidence of past shipwrecks, and climb on dunes that rise 300 feet from the shore, this is the place.

This park preserves the natural beauty of the lake, a remnant of the once-wild shores that can only be enjoyed if you plan on a lot of time and some personal effort. If you are bringing young children, the hikes can be too long, so you will want to choose carefully to ensure they have fun and find inspiration rather than frustration. For example, you can visit the lighthouse and Coast Guard station in neighboring Grand Marais before you hike in to Au Sable

Lighthouse, a 1½-mile one-way hike that will require some water, food, and encouragement. Then you can hike the beach from Hurricane River Campground and see parts of old shipwrecks. Ask the kids why the lighthouses are needed.

The Twelvemile Beach Campground is the best beach for the children to play on. They do not need to walk far, and the sand is wonderful for all the castles and construction that beaches inspire. If you are a camper, it is a great place to extend your visit and enjoy the fun of not having to get in and out of the car—driving is seldom a child's favorite activity. In addition, there are campgrounds at Hurricane River and Little Beaver Lake. Then you can end the day with a campfire, roasted marshmallows, and a few stories.

There are some great shore hikes to take, too, like Miner's Falls and the boardwalk at Sand Point Marsh, as well as both the White Pine and the White Birch nature trails. Check out the short walk to Miner's Castle, too. Short, easy terrain and rewarding exercise! With older grandchildren you want to make sure you take the longer hike to Chapel Rock, where the rocks have eroded, creating an almost mystical formation. This is a good walk that isn't very demanding, but it is longer and young attention spans can wander.

To enjoy the sand dunes, let your grandchildren climb up and down and wear themselves out, or you can hike to Log Slide, which is an easy walk with a magnificent view of the dunes and the lake. And if you are not camping or hiking but just want to have an excellent beach walk or just sit and watch the sunset, be sure to visit Sand Point.

Bonding & Bridging

There are many great reasons to go boating with your grandchildren—enjoying the sun and breeze, exploring new areas, sharing time together. However, there is an even better reason for going by boat here. Pictured Rocks offers great opportunities for exploring the shore and the landscape away from the lake, but it cannot give you a view of the "pictured" rocks themselves. A boat can, and does, give you the true feeling of this park and lets you really connect with Lake Superior. Bring food, a blanket in case the breeze is too cold, and a windbreaker. Then let the captain guide the trip while you guide your grandchildren to an excellent adventure.

A WORD TO THE WISE:

You can hardly go wrong at this park. It truly offers a superb set of options, but you have to pace yourself. Walking on sand is tough; climbing the dunes can be exhausting. Choose your activities according to both your physical ability and those of your grandchildren. If you overextend either way, you lose the chance to go away with pleasant memories. Look at the options we have listed, go to the Visitor Center, and spend time with guidebooks.

When we stay within our own limits we always have a better time. If you just want to observe and end up swimming, go to Grand Marais and enjoy its sheltered beach and natural sand harbor. If you want to take boats out, go to Munising. There are many options, and hopefully you can return to do those things you weren't able to do on the first visit. It is not important that you do everything, but it is important that the things you choose contribute to a wonderful time.

AGE OF GRANDCHILD: 3 and up, depending upon the activities you choose.

BEST SEASON: Summer

CONTACT: Pictured Rocks National Lakeshore, Munising, MI 49862-0040; (906) 387-3700; Park: www.nps.gov/piro

Pictured Rocks Cruises: www.picturedrocks.com

ALSO CHECK OUT:

Grand Island National Recreation Area: www.grandislandup.com

Sleeping Bear Dunes National Lakeshore: www.nps.gov/slbe

Few things are more delightful than grandchildren fighting over your lap. **Doug Larson**

34

Marquette Maritime Museum

In a state with extensive coastlines, it is hard to find a more colorful history than that of shipping and lighthouses. Think of the motifs that we use for decorating homes, restaurants, and tourist areas; your grandchildren know about lighthouses even if they have never been to the coast.

The Marquette Maritime Museum is part of a harbor complex that includes ore docks, sailboat moorings, and a dynamic park system. You can walk this area, let your curiosity flow, and enjoy the brisk breezes that flow from Lake Superior. It is a place that invites playfulness and observation, and it is a natural lead-in to a museum associated with a Coast Guard station.

The museum has a variety of exhibits that include stories of American Indians who crossed these waters in birchbark canoes as well as a diorama of the Marquette shoreline. There is a fishing shack, a pilot house, and a story about the Coast Guard and their heroics, shipwrecks, and lifesaving. The museum is

small, and it will be just right for engaging the children before visiting the lighthouse. Before going out to the lighthouse, let your grandchildren view the area through a real periscope; don't miss it: this is a wonderful experience that is found in very few museums. Think of the way submariners see the world!

This square, red lighthouse is unusual in both shape and color, and it stands out against the dark rocks of this small peninsula. Thanks to a 30-year lease with the Coast Guard, the museum allows you to walk out on the rocks and through the building. This is the second lighthouse to be built here. The first was built in 1853; the current structure was constructed in 1866; the second story was added in 1909. The basic structure was part of a concerted effort to build lighthouses on the Great Lakes. Its original design was lost over the decades through additions and repairs. Coast Guard families lived in the lighthouse as late as 1998, 145 years after the first light was put into use.

The lighthouse is the oldest structure in Marquette, which emphasizes the fact that the city exists because of the lake and harbor; the community was built from the lake inland. To understand this better, you need to walk the boardwalk out to the end of the peninsula and look back at the light, the harbor, and the city. For many, this is the true highlight of the experience.

Bonding & Bridging

The museum is a low-key operation that shares seafaring stories; one of the highlights is its collection of lighthouse lenses. If you were to compare the various lights in the building and in your life, you would see that we use light in many ways. Help your grandchildren see the difference between the directed beam of a flashlight and the light from a lamp. Compare the bulbs. The flashlight seems to give off more light because it is concentrated, while a lamp is actually lighting a wider area, but the light is diffused and less brilliant in any direction.

If you help your grandchildren explore concepts like this, you are also helping them to understand science, invention and purpose. Which kind of light would help the ship in distress? Why would the lens be important to the lighthouse?

A WORD TO THE WISE:

August is Maritime Month in Marquette. The Upper Peninsula Children's Museum, the Marquette Maritime Museum, the Lake Superior Theater, and the city combine to offer plays, seafood meals, boat rides, storytelling, an open house at the Coast Guard station, yacht races, and children's events.

This is a colorful time and one that can really enhance your experience. When you can combine festivals with your visit, the children can blend the things they see with hands-on experience, which is proven to have a strong educational effect. These organized events also help you keep the children engaged and allow you to be their playmate and fellow explorer.

AGE OF GRANDCHILD: All

BEST SEASON: Summer

CONTACT: 300 N Lake Shore Blvd., Marquette, MI 49855; (906) 226-2006; http://mqtmaritimemuseum.com/

ALSO CHECK OUT:

Fort Gratiot Lighthouse: www.phmuseum.org/fort-gratiot-lighthouse/

Granite Island Light Station: www.graniteisland.com

Great Lakes Shipwreck Museum: www.shipwreckmuseum.com

Point Betsie Lighthouse: www.pointbetsie.org

Sable Points Lighthouse Keepers Association: http://splka.org

You're never too old to become younger. MAE WEST

35

Michigan Iron Industry Museum

It's hard to imagine that a little valley on the Carp River in the Upper Peninsula of Michigan could be an important iron mining site that helped our country construct skyscrapers and the railroad tracks that cross the continent. But here it is, a historic site and a wonderful museum for grandparents and grandchildren to begin to explore one of our country's "big stories."

The museum is constantly adding hands-on displays, ways for the visitor to discover the unique history of this location and ways to learn about the lives of the miners who provided the real power for the industry. This is the

site of the first iron forge in the Lake Superior region, and this area, along with Minnesota's iron range, was one of the major centers of the North American iron mining industry.

Explore the hands-on exhibits and watch the introductory film to add dimension to the exploration. Coming here helps you understand iron mining, and also helps you gain a perspective on mining in its many forms. The U.P. is also home to copper mines, so the relationship of the people to the landscape is tied to the rocks, the trees, and the waters!

The main exhibit is a little like a maze, with twisting pathways leading you along your journey. It discusses mining history, the role the Great Lakes played, and features a family album that helps you understand the people who worked these mines. Never forget the story of the people. These were immigrants, as most of our ancestors were. They came to support their families, and they worked hard and sacrificed for the industries that grew on their shoulders.

After you absorb the images, the information, and the ideas, take the final journey into a simulated mine tunnel. This is very well done and leaves a strong impression about the experience of being a miner. Think about what the work was like and how difficult it must have been.

The museum has two outdoor interpretive trails for visitors to enjoy (both are less than a half-mile). The River Overlook Trail has a wooden walkway that leads through the treetops. An observation deck has signs telling the story of the Carp River Forge, which operated from 1848 to 1855. The trail meanders through the forest above the Carp River leading to a section that depicts American Indian use of the environment before the arrival of Europeans. The Geology Trail leads from the main parking lot over a ridge where trail walkers can learn about geological features and early iron mining exploration. Near the end of the trail is a vista where the Tilden Iron Mine can be seen nine miles off in the distance.

A WORD TO THE WISE:

Cliffs Shaft Mine in Ishpeming is nearby and should be added to this visit. For a hundred years men went down to the mine and brought out ore. Now there is also a mineral exhibit and some of the most spectacular buildings in ore country. After seeing these, your grandchildren will be amazed by the size of this historic site and it will add perspective that goes far beyond what we can tell them or show them in photographs. These two combine for an excellent day full of adventure.

AGE OF GRANDCHILD: 8 and up

BEST SEASON: Summer

CONTACT: Michigan Iron Industry Museum, 73 Forge Rd., Negaunee, MI 49866; (906) 475-7857; www.michigan.gov/mhc/0,4726,7-282-61080_62658---,00.html

Cliffs Shaft Mine, 501 W Euclid St., Ishpeming, MI 49849; (906) 485-1882; www.michigan.org/property/cliffs-shaft-mine-museum/

ALSO CHECK OUT:

Coppertown: www.uppermichigan.com/coppertown/main.html

Delaware Mine: www.delawarecopperminetours.com

Menominee Range Historical Museum: www.menomineemuseum.com

Quincy Mine: www.quincymine.com

Family faces are magic mirrors. Looking at people who belong to us, we see the past, present and future. GAIL LUMET BUCKLEY

36

U.S. Ski & Snowboard Hall of Fame and Museum

In a city that is known for iron mining and is closer to three Great Lakes than it is to a mountain, you might not expect to find the U.S. Ski and Snowboard Hall of Fame and Museum, but here it is, and it is both appropriate and fascinating. Over 100 years ago the National Skiing Association got its start in Ishpeming and that was the true birth of organized skiing. While skiing became popular in the mountains, the immigrant settlers in the land of lake-effect snow really helped popularize the sport in the U.S.

As one might expect in any hall of fame, there are many photographs and biographies of famous people. Yet skiers seldom obtain the fame that many professional athletes achieve, so the names are seldom as recognizable as one of

your other sports heroes. Unless you and your family are really skiing aficionados, there will only be a few people you will recognize, but you'll certainly recognize some names you've heard during the Olympics or on the news.

But if you and your grandchildren enjoy getting out on the slopes, you will find some fun stories on the plaques, if you take time to sample a few. Of course, you'll really connect with the displays, which feature a huge collection of skis with everything from wood skis with leather straps to the vibrant colors and forms in today's ski design. Try to get your grandchild to imagine what the old skis were like, although the history your grandchild might enjoy the most is the collection of snowboards. For many of us, the snowboards seem like a brand new item, but you will be impressed with the designs.

Then there are displays that show you old-time fashions—yes, you probably wore some of these, but you don't have to admit it to your grandchildren. Skiing is a fashion sport, and it is fun to look back at these wardrobe classics. Contrast those outfits and equipment with what we have today, or take a look at the display with Vikings wearing the sport's original gear.

There is also a tribute to the 10th Mountain Division, a heroic division of the military that engaged in some very dramatic events in World War II and which is still active today.

Bonding & Bridging

Today we have the X Games and the Olympics and other enjoyable venues for skiing, but skis allowed our ancestors to settle the snowy country. Try to imagine what northern winters would have been like without skis or snowshoes. It is good to see how people used the materials at hand to create the tools they needed. Snow is a great medium for lots of our fun, but it is also an obstacle to survival. Here, you can talk about weather, personal challenges, ingenuity, and adapting to your surroundings. If you live in a northern climate, you should enjoy winter and to do that means to learn to play, as well as work, with the elements. You might consider a dogsled ride or a visit to the Subaru Noquemanon Ski Marathon in Marquette to complement this discussion and experience a unique shared adventure in the spirit of winter.

A WORD TO THE WISE:

We hope that you can enjoy the lake-effect snows and the abundance of skiing opportunities, including both cross-country and downhill options. To stay in the know, check the state's ski condition website before you go. Porcupine Mountains Wildnerness State Park includes opportunities for both cross-country and downhill skiing. In addition, the national forests, state parks, and communities often maintain trails, and the commercial downhill ski operators all have their own websites to check out.

When you're out skiing, don't be surprised if you find your grandchildren going a different route. Ask them to do a run or two with you first and set a time and place to meet. If you are cross-country skiing, make sure that everyone has a map and can read it. Bring water, some food, and a first aid kit.

AGE OF GRANDCHILD: 10 and up

BEST SEASON: Winter, when you are enjoying the snow yourself.

CONTACT: 610 Palms Ave., Ishpeming, MI 49849; (906) 485-6323; www.skihall.com

ALSO CHECK OUT:

Michigan Cross-Country Skiing: www.michigan.org/skiing/cross-country

Michigan Downhill Skiing: www.michigan.org/skiing/downhill/

Michigan Snow Report: www.onthesnow.com/michigan/skireport.html

All things are connected, like the blood which connects one family. Whatever befalls the Earth befalls the children of the Earth. CHIEF SEATTLE

Sylvania Wilderness

Exploring the wilderness often requires a heavy backpack filled with food, a tent, and everything else you might need for your trip, and you might have to carry it over rugged terrain. While that is invigorating, it is also a quick way to separate the strong from the weak, the fast from the slow, and the young from the old.

The Sylvania Wilderness is much smaller than the famed Boundary Waters Canoe Area Wilderness in Minnesota, but combined with the adjacent Sylvania Recreation Area, it provides 18,327 acres of forested beauty with

large red and white pines, as well as 34 named lakes, and the landscape is a habitat haven for bald eagles, ospreys, loons, and wolves.

Canoes at the Sylvania Wilderness are equalizers. Two paddlers balance one another's strengths. You can converse quietly, set a comfortable pace, and let the boat support the weight of the food and supplies. While some people relish moving camp to cover big distances and seeing lots of lakes, it should not be the goal of a grandparent/grandchild trip. Pick your lakes wisely, avoid the worst times for insects, and concentrate on finding a campsite with a nice beach and stay there.

Explore one lake. Build a nice fire. Share stories. Go fishing. Work together and allow the grandchildren to develop the skills to return. Look at the moss, the rocks, the lichens. Hike into the woods, bring good food. Look at the stars.

Children love swimming. Let them float in their life jackets. Settle in and let the country become a part of your shared experience. Let the grandchildren develop a sense of place. Let them draw, paint, write, and take pictures. Encourage their observations rather than giving them your perspective. Put a soft Frisbee in your pack and add a hidden treat for each day.

There are too many outfitters to list, but check with the U.S. Forest Service to get an idea of where to start. Let the kids help make the plans; decide what to bring and why, what are good foods for such a trip, and what route you want to explore. Let them help you draw up the rules for camp. Use anticipation as part of the experience. You might just find that this is an adventure you will want to repeat annually!

Bonding & Bridging

Some of the experiences we have had in our lifetime are disappearing. We call them "endangered" experiences. These include—silence, solitude, wildness, the joy of being alone, and the dark night sky. As grandparents, we can remember when these were not so hard to find, and we need to do all we can to keep these experiences alive for future generations. Grandchildren who do not see us every day may view us as ancient as the trees, rocks, and waters that abound in this landscape. We become a part of the background of their life and their planet. Through us, the world can become alive and positive. While they may make demands of parents for things they "want" and "need," they are more willing to investigate the grandparents' world and they might find that playing with rocks and sticks is as satisfying as any electronic gadget.

A WORD TO THE WISE:

On a very calm evening, put on the life jackets (everyone—not just the grandchildren) and float out in your canoe to where you can watch the sun set and the stars rise. This is an event that every grandparent and grandchild should share—and when you paddle back silently, look at the stars reflected in the water. This is truly inter-generational space travel.

AGE OF GRANDCHILD: 10 minimum and no limit on the upper end. We had friends who guided in their 60s and knew others who took an annual trip well into their 80s. Only you can judge these limits.

BEST SEASON: Late summer and early fall, when the insects aren't as bad.

CONTACT: Ottawa National Forest, E23989 US-2 East, Watersmeet, MI; (906) 358-4551; www.fs.usda.gov/recarea/ottawa/recarea/?recid=12331 Permit reservations: www.recreation.gov

ALSO CHECK OUT:

Au Sable River Association: www.ausableriver.org

Manistee River Trail:
www.michigantrailmaps.com/member-profile/3/127/

Pere Marquette National Scenic River:
www.fs.usda.gov/recarea/hmnf/recarea/?recid=18608

Whatever you love is beautiful; love comes first, beauty follows. The greater your capacity for love, the more beauty you find in the world. JANE SMILEY

38

Porcupine Mountains Wilderness State Park

Sometimes the name "State Park" can be misleading. State parks tend to be regional or statewide assets. They are beautiful, ecologically important, and a wonderful resource for recreation and discovery. But some state parks are much more than that. They are like national parks on a waiting list, areas that are regionally important, and important on a global scale, too.

This is true old-growth forest. Here you can find ancient, massive trees like those that greeted the Anishinaabe (Ojibwa) and the subsequent pioneers. The Ojibwa looked at the massive rock ridges here and the forest that surrounded them and referred to the area as the "Porcupine Mountains."

And this park is huge; 60,000 acres might not mean anything to you, but rest assured, that's a lot of room. On a given visit, you'll only be able to sample the park's wildness and diversity with your grandchildren.

There are 85 miles of trails for the adventuresome grandparent/grandchildren, but many magnificent places that are also easy to reach. One example is the overlook (escarpment) at Lake of the Clouds, which includes a minimum of walking and a maximum of "aahs."

Other highlights include the magnificent coastline on the Lake Superior Shoreline Trail and the Presque Isle area on the west side. Here, trails allow

you to explore rapids and waterfalls just before the water flows into the lake. At Union Bay, a sandy beach awaits swimmers and sand castle builders, while the Union Mine trail near the Visitor Center will help you explore the mining history of the park.

Then you can go to Summit Peak— it is only 1,958 feet high and is the highest peak in the park, but numbers do not tell it all. Lake Superior is 602 feet above sea level at the surface, and after a half-mile walk from Summit Peak Road, you and your grandchildren are 1,300 feet above the lake. Here, you can see for miles in all directions and witness a panorama usually reserved for hawks and eagles.

No matter which way you go, watch for birds, bears, and blossoms. This is a rich landscape where nature provides rewards to explorers willing to observe and enjoy the park at a leisurely pace.

Bonding & Bridging

If your grandchildren are old enough, you might want to talk to them about the forces that shaped our Earth. Consider the oceans, the movement of continents and their collisions, the power of continental glaciers, and the fury of volcanoes. Consider how much our landscapes are shaped by the seemingly benign forces of sun, water, freezing, and melting.

Geologists are people who read the stories the Earth has to tell, and can predict where we can find minerals and other natural resources, where we can build safely, and how to interpret fossils and the land. None of us really understands what it means to be millions or billions of years old, but we do get a sense of our own place amid the history of creation when we examine how old the world around us really is. To help make this more clear, head to the Visitor Center and then make your way to the escarpment, where your grandchildren can begin to see the strength and power of the forces that shape the Earth.

A WORD TO THE WISE:

The Visitor Center has great displays that help tell the story and provides visuals of the animals that live here. We all know it is hard to see animals in the wild; we have to work at it, be quiet, be out early and late in the day, and be prepared with binoculars and field guides. Even then we may see only a faint track or a brief movement. In the Visitor Center, displays, maps, and even the books in the gift store can provide the basis for your hiking and learning. Take advantage of this assistance and engage in discovery with your grandchild.

AGE OF GRANDCHILD: All

BEST SEASON: All

CONTACT: 33303 Headquarters Rd., Ontonagon, MI 49953; (906-884-2047), (906) 885-5275; Visitor Center: www.porcupineup.com

ALSO CHECK OUT:

Isle Royale National Park: www.nps.gov/isro_

Pictured Rocks National Lakeshore: www.nps.gov/piro

Sleeping Bear Dunes National Lakeshore: www.nps.gov/slbe

Tahquamenon Falls State Park:
www.michigandnr.com/parksandtrails/Details.aspx?id=428&type=SPRK

You are the sun, Grandma, you are the sun in my life. Kitty Tsui

39

Keweenaw National Historical Park

History is hard to confine. This is true of the story of the Keweenaw Peninsula and the historic copper mining that established the Upper Peninsula as a source of this country's wealth. At one time this landscape was responsible for 80 percent of the copper being produced in the U.S., and as a result, families moved here from faraway countries, railroad lines were built, cities were constructed, and mines probed the dark depths of the Earth.

Many of these stories are now told at Keweenaw Historical Park, but unlike most parks, this one is a series of locations scattered across the land like a child's connect-the-dots book. Because of this arrangement, it's easier to make the historical connections to help your grandchildren see a vivid picture of this unique story in the process.

The Quincy Mine & Hoist is a good place to begin. With lots of historic buildings and ruins, the site still gives you a feeling of the size of the operation. Even more importantly, you're allowed to go into the buildings and enter the mine; this will help your grandchildren forge a real connection to the life and times of the miners. There are pieces of copper to look at, massive cables, and many other artifacts. The mine once reached 9,260 feet, and visitors on tour can go down 700 feet to the seventh level and explore a 2,400-foot section of it. There are 85 levels below the seventh level, but the these are all filled with water today.

You will descend and return by a cog railway train that handles the steep outside grade. Cog railways are rare and provide an additional sense of fun to the exploration. At the shaft, a tractor-pulled wagon will take your family into the darkness underground. The tunnel is lit, but expect the guide to let you experience the darkness that the miners knew, for at least a few seconds.

When you finish the ride it is time to go to Calumet, the aboveground world of the miners and their families and the businesses that depended upon them. Here, you'll find wonderful historic structures protected and still functioning, with such kid-friendly options as the Upper Peninsula Firefighters Memorial Museum, and musical and theater performances in the old Calumet Theatre.

Bonding & Bridging

Exploring the mine, it is possible for you to explore a number of difficult concepts. Good stories told properly can stay with a child forever—that's why we still have so many oral stories with us. For instance, tell them that all resources are limited—ask what happens when the mine runs out of minerals—to the people who work there, the people who sold things to the workers, to the communities and the families? Should we be careful with limited resources and how we use them? What are we using now that might be running out? Why does a person work underground 8–10 hours a day? What motivates that person? What kind of job would you like? What do you have to do to get the work you want?

A WORD TO THE WISE:

This historic park does not own all the historic sites on the Upper Peninsula, but it does cooperate with many to allow you even more great experiences. For example, the Delaware Copper Mine is a walking tour that takes you 100 feet underground and lets you see pure veins of copper. The site also includes llamas, deer, model trains, and antique engines. Copper World is a commercial operation in an 1869 wood-framed house in Calumet where your grandchildren can see copper in many forms. You can also find excellent minerals in the collection at the A.E. Seaman Mineral Museum at Michigan Tech.

AGE OF GRANDCHILD: 5 and up

BEST SEASON: Summer and fall

CONTACT: 25970 Red Jacket Rd., Calumet, MI 49913; (906) 337-3168; www.nps.gov/kewe

ALSO CHECK OUT:

A.E. Seaman Mineral Museum: www.museum.mtu.edu

Calumet Theatre: www.calumettheatre.com

Chassell Historical Organization: www.chassellhistory.org

Coppertown Mining Museum: www.keweenawheritagesites.org/site-coppertown.php

Delaware Copper Mine: www.delawarecopperminetours.com

Old Victoria Historical Site: www.ontonagon.net/oldvictoria

Through my grandmother's eyes, I can see more clearly the way things used to be, the way things ought to be, and most important of all, the way things really are. ED CUNNINGHAM

40

Fort Wilkins Historic State Park

The 150-mile Keweenaw Peninsula extends into a rugged freshwater sea—Lake Superior—and ends at the remote town of Copper Harbor. The historic Fort Wilkins was built for a battle that was never fought. This is not a place you get to by accident, because it is not on the way to anything except a boat ride to Isle Royale National Park. But don't let that stop your discovery. You might just find that once you get there you won't want to go anywhere else.

Air-conditioned by the lake, wild because of its isolation, and inspiring because of its rocky highlands, sandy and rocky shorelines, hidden bays, thick forests, and abundant waterfalls, this is a landscape that allows you to share the wonder of remoteness with your grandchildren.

Fort Wilkins Historic State Park is much more than the historic military fort. This forested area lies between Lake Superior and Lake Fanny Hooe, which,

besides being a beautiful lake with a strange name, makes the fort feel like it is on an island.

Fort Wilkins is in great shape, with displays in each of the buildings that help you capture the feeling of fort life. Built in 1844, this was a peaceful place created to calm tensions between the copper miners and American Indians, a problem that never became reality. Mostly these men just served their time and, according to the commandant who struggled to instill a work ethic in them, they did not do too well. Think about what this assignment must have been like for the men. This was not a tourist destination, but a point at the edge of the forest frontier on the shores of a wild lake. There was no easy route in or out and certainly no way to get support if there was trouble. This was isolation, and they probably did not enjoy the scenery the way we do today.

To keep your visit filled with pleasure, you can go fishing or catch a small boat to the lighthouse, go rock collecting on the cobblestone beaches, and explore the dunes near Eagle Harbor.

Bonding & Bridging ⌇⌇⌇⌇⌇⌇⌇⌇⌇⌇⌇⌇⌇⌇⌇⌇⌇⌇⌇

In many ways this fort is a good place to examine military life. We study battles and wars, but the military has many more roles to play. Men and women do many tasks that are neither heroic nor dangerous but are essential, and we place our military in positions where we discourage war and unrest. War itself is a failure in human relationships and communications.

Help your grandchildren understand the importance of the military to our nation, but also help them understand that peace is the real mission of military service, something we too often forget. Also ask your grandchildren what life would have been like here beyond the reach of family and friends, without telephone and television. How would people get what they needed, and even more important, what did they really need?

A WORD TO THE WISE:

This wonderful natural paradise includes one of the most scenic roads in Michigan—Brockway Mountain Drive. The steep grade lifts you quickly from the lake level and provides the kind of feelings you expect on a scenic drive in the Appalachians.

The road is short with lots of pull-outs as it follows the ridgeline of an ancient geologic fold that slides beneath Lake Superior, only to reappear as Isle Royale National Park. From the highest points you can look for a glimpse of the island park, or dream about exploring the inland lakes, streams, and forests. It is also great place for bird watching.

AGE OF GRANDCHILD: 10 and up

BEST SEASON: Summer

CONTACT: 15223 US-41, Copper Harbor, MI 49918; (906) 289-4215; www.michigandnr.com/parksandtrails/Details.aspx?type=SPRK&id=419

ALSO CHECK OUT:

Colonial Fort Michilimackinac: www.mackinacparks.com/parks-and-attractions/colonial-michilimackinac

Fort Mackinac: www.mackinacparks.com/parks-and-attractions/fort-mackinac

Historic Fort Wayne Coalition: www.historicfortwaynecoalition.com

It's amazing how grandparents seem so young once you become one. UNKNOWN

41

Isle Royale National Park

This is not a people place, and that is what makes it so special. Not everyone goes to Isle Royale; in fact, it is one of the least visited of our national parks. Then again, few places are so remote and wild, and this is the essence of this experience.

For grandparents who value nature, wilderness, self-reliance, exercise, fresh air, the opportunity to withdraw from crowds and the artificial attraction of shops and trinkets—this is the place to be. If you are tired of cell phones and the Internet, electronic games, and gadgetry, there are few places that can remove you from those influences like this 45-mile-long island in the midst of Lake Superior's cold and watery solitude.

When you want to go back to nature and feel the rhythm of the land, this is the place to come. There are several ways to get there, but none that includes driving. From Michigan's Upper Peninsula you can take a boat from

Houghton or Copper Harbor that takes three and a half to five hours to cross the lake, or catch a seaplane and cover the distance in 35–45 minutes. Either way, the voyage will give you a sense of the remoteness of this landscape. This is important for perspective and adds to the mystery that will help your grandchildren get into the wilderness mood.

After you cover the distance, you will arrive in Rock Harbor. You will arrive to a feeling of bustling energy and see the people staying at the Rock Harbor Lodge, the only non-camping option on the island, and park staff doing their work. Rock Harbor is the closest you will come to a city in this park.

Now you have the choice—a backcountry visit or one at the lodge? Choose the one that fits your personal skills and interests and those of your grandchildren. Even though this park belongs to the wildlife and the paths that you take are the same ones they follow, there are options when the pack is too heavy and the trail too long.

These include a wonderful day hike of 4.3 miles to Scoville Point that provides options for discovering the island's ecology. Or take the 3.8-mile loop to Suzy's Cave—a wave-washed sea cave (arch). Or catch a boat to explore Tobin's Harbor and watch the loons, or canoe to little Raspberry Island—a 2-mile round-trip.

Bonding & Bridging

If you can share *this* park, you will have something so unusual and dramatic that it will stay with your grandchildren for the rest of their lives. You do not need to do anything extra. You just need to be there. Like the camaraderie of the athletic field, the sense here of shared success heightens the feelings and deepens the memories. The sound of the waves, the wind in the trees, the moose and wolf tracks on the field are like spices to a wild child, and when you share your warm soup or cocoa and talk about what you just did, your grandchildren's future reflections will be tempered by that moment.

A WORD TO THE WISE:

If you are like us, you may have been able to walk these trails with only the normal discomfort of backpacking when you were young, but the addition of weight to your back is no longer just hard work—now it is difficult and demanding. You do not have to prove anything to your grandchildren; you have a free pass with them. Just choose what is appropriate and enjoy every step and every minute. When we put undue stress on ourselves, we place a burden on our companions and we change our personalities and our pleasure. Do some walks while wearing a pack before you go. Find out and accept what you can and should do.

AGE OF GRANDCHILD: 10 and up

BEST SEASON: Summer

CONTACT: Headquarters: 800 E Lakeshore Dr., Houghton, MI; (906) 482-0984; www.nps.gov/isro

ALSO CHECK OUT:

Isle Royale Ranger III: www.nps.gov/isro/planyourvisit/ranger-iii-info.htm

Isle Royale Seaplanes: www.isleroyaleseaplanes.com

The Isle Royale Line: www.isleroyale.com

Beaver Island: www.beaverisland.org

Grand Island National Recreation Area: www.grandislandferry.com

Pictured Rocks National Lakeshore: www.nps.gov/piro

There is no other door to knowledge than the door Nature opens. And there is no truth but the truth we discover in Nature. Luther Burbank

42

Amtrak

I have always loved riding trains, ever since my mom took my brother and me on a trip to Chicago when I was about 8. The sound of the wheels clacking on the rails, the rocking of the cars, as if we were on the ocean, made an adventure of grand proportions, even though we were only traveling from Minneapolis. Arriving and departing from depots with high marble ceilings added to the grandeur of the experience. There was glamour (a dining car) and wonder (the dome car at night) on those trips, and I have never lost the desire to ride the rails.

Luckily, in Michigan, there are still lots of options for train travel. Three major routes travel from Chicago to Kalamazoo, Port Huron, and Detroit and can take you to 23 Michigan cities. These trains are The Pere Marquette, with

daily service between Grand Rapids and Chicago; The Wolverine, with daily service between Pontiac and Chicago; and The Blue Water, with daily service between Port Huron and Chicago. The longest trip is six hours and thirty minutes, and with the flexibility of the railroad car, this is an easy way to travel.

Today's children, especially little boys, it seems, have a great fascination with one particular train—Thomas the Tank Engine. Maybe you remember the Lionel set you got for Christmas and played with for several years. Maybe you still have it and are ready to set it up again for a new generation of train buffs. This experience might rekindle that joy in your grandchildren, and in you.

Riding the train today is a very comfortable experience. The seats are twice as roomy as those in airplanes, and you can get up and walk around whenever you like—no seat belts. There are fold-down tables and even electrical outlets near the seats, so you can plug in computers or other digital devices if you grow tired of watching the great scenery. And that has always been a big part of the pleasure of riding the train—traveling at a speed that allows us to see the landscape and the lives of the people we're passing. The trains go through backyards and industrial areas, past farmsteads and small towns. You can just barely hear the whistle in these well-insulated cars, but it blows whenever you cross over roads, with the warning arms down. Wave to the people who are standing by the side of the tracks or in their cars waiting for the train to pass; you are on a time machine.

Plan your train trip with your grandkids. Show them the different routes and ask them where they'd like to go. This also means you need to look up information about the destination and find out what you can do in that town before you catch the train back home. If you have a map to plot your trip, use it to research the towns you will go through and bring it along to keep track of your progress.

Planning for a journey is half the fun and builds anticipation for the trip. If you have a train set at home, set it up before or after the trip and relive the fun. And talk to the children about the way you traveled in the past and how it differs from today. Did your family have just one car? Did that seem sufficient? Ask them whether they think travel will be different in the future. Encourage them to use their imagination to project how they will travel in 30 years.

A WORD TO THE WISE:

Amtrak has had a reputation for being late, but it is working hard to correct this image. Part of it has to do with the availability of tracks, since freight trains often move on the same routes. With all the recent snafus and frustrations with air travel, trains are looking better all the time. At least you can get up and walk around and use the bathrooms on a train, even when you're not moving. Pack snacks or sandwiches for your trip, in case you are delayed. The Dining Car and Lounge Car serve food, but it is more expensive than you may want to pay. Bring along games to play, too, since this is a great setting for conversation and one-on-one competition. The Lounge Car has domed windows and nice tables where you can sit and play games.

AGE OF GRANDCHILD: 3 and up

BEST SEASON: Any

CONTACT: (800) 872-7245; www.amtrak.com/michigan-services-train

ALSO CHECK OUT:

Little River Railroad, Coldwater to Quincy: www.littleriverrailroad.com

Michigan Transit Museum, Mount Clemens: www.michigantransitmuseum.org

Southern Michigan Railroad Society: www.southernmichiganrailroad.com

Toonerville Trolley, Riverboat and Train Ride to Tahquamenon Falls: www.trainandboattours.com

Our children grow up so fast. Maybe grandchildren are God's way of giving us a second chance at participating in the miracle of life. UNKNOWN

43

Art Museums

What child doesn't enjoy coloring books, doodling with crayons or markers, molding clay, building sand castles, or building with Legos? These activities are all art! They require creativity and expression. Great art is something different, but great art and children's art are both part of the same spectrum. Both should be enjoyed and celebrated, and where's a better place to do so than at an art museum?

The Detroit Institute of Art (DIA) and the Grand Rapids Art Museum (GRAM) are amazing treasure troves of artifacts, creations, colors, design, and inspiration. But it takes time and creative visits to allow children to enjoy and appreciate what they see. Walking through a museum can be overwhelming, especially for young ones. Don't overdo it; trying to see too much in one visit can overload children and adults alike, so make short and frequent visits. Children are challenged by both the quiet observation and the "no touch" policies. In a short visit these can be exciting elements, but if a visit is too long it can frustrate them and taint the opportunity to build a foundation for the future.

Some works of art obviously interest children. At the DIA it is easy to see how a knight's armor could capture a child's imagination, and how Diego Rivera's massive murals might overwhelm everyone with their size and detail. But how do you explore the other artwork? In an age when pirate movies are so popular, it's often good to begin with the idea of an artistic treasure hunt. Look for similar themes or objects throughout the museum. The DIA provides one example of this, and small booklets challenge kids to look for various themes throughout the art collection. For example, the "Yikes!" booklet centers on eerie thrills, "Take a Hike" emphasizes nature, and "Game Day" encourages kids to find athletics in the art. In addition to these themed visits, there are "I spy" clues on the walls of exhibit rooms. Your job is to act as an art detective and use the clue to find an object that would fit the clue. To do so, you must examine the art in the room and find the correct answer. If you're stumped, the answer is under the flipboard.

Bonding & Bridging

One grandmother told us she used the stories she read with her granddaughter to provide a theme for their visit. Like the treasure hunt idea, this helps connect the granddaughter directly to the experience of observing art. They look at the artwork together and once the granddaughter has found something that fits the theme, the grandmother asks questions. Does it look real? What is the picture about—does it have its own story? If possible, they look for additional art with the theme and look at the differences and similarities—a wonderful learning exercise and a way to share. If you feel intimidated about explaining art, use one of the museum's audio tours. They have designed one just for kids ages 8–14.

A WORD TO THE WISE:

Both museums offer special activities for children, and these can help you share the world of art in a creative way. For example, the Grand Rapids Art Museum's "Purposeful Play + Artful Learning" is designed for ages 4 and under! There is also a drop-in studio where you might learn about sunprints or participate in another art project. The Detroit Institute of Art has drop-in workshops that are hands-on and feature everything from paper dolls to kites! It also has special music events. Check out both museums to find the activity that suits your family.

AGE OF GRANDCHILD: 4 and older

BEST SEASON: All

CONTACT: Detroit Institute of Arts, 5200 Woodward Ave., Detroit, MI 48202; (313) 833-7900; www.dia.org

Grand Rapids Art Museum, 101 Monroe Ctr. NW, Grand Rapids, MI 49503; (616) 831-1000; www.artmuseumgr.org

ALSO CHECK OUT:

Eli and Edythe Broad Art Museum: https://broadmuseum.msu.edu/

Frederik Meijer Gardens & Sculpture Park: www.meijergardens.org

Krasl Art Center: www.krasl.org

Marshall M. Fredericks Sculpture Garden & Museum: www.marshallfredericks.org

When grandparents enter the door,
discipline flies out the window. OGDEN NASH

44

Beaches

Who doesn't like a beach? Talk about a place to bond and a perfect picture of the state of Michigan with its 3,288 miles of Great Lakes coastline and 11,000 inland lakes!

Nothing excites our grandchildren like water. They want to wade in it, throw rocks in it, splash, sit, float boats, and build castles in the sand, and nothing more elaborate than this. Your job is to keep them safe and encourage their imagination. If we were to survey our grandchildren about what they'd like to do, we believe the beach would be their first choice.

Sandy beaches provide the ideal construction material for young designers. A small shovel, a pail, a few plastic toys, and time combine to make forts, roads, castles, and adventures. Get down and build a castle (or start it and let

them take over). This can take hours and your presence alone will make this more fun for the child. And plan for them to get wet whether they go swimming or not. Beaches are the intersection of water and land and who doesn't want to cross that boundary now and then? Splashing is one of the great pleasures of a beach walk, following the wave line, trying to get close to shorebirds, rousting the gulls, and letting the waves chase you.

Along some rocky beaches the term "beachcomber" takes on extra meaning as you search for treasures like the famous Petoskey stone (pieces of an ancient coral formation). Bring a cooler for the all-day adventures, with lots of liquids and some yummy, but nutritious, picnic food. Sun and too many sweets can make for a bad ending to a good day.

Finally, make sure some of your beach visits include a sunset. Sitting and watching the sun slip into the water is not only beautiful, it is also a perfect time for contemplation and quiet. Take in the colors, observe the clouds, and if it is a fine sunset, the sun will not mind ovation and applause.

Bonding & Bridging

There are many ways to play. Playing in snow is one way, piles of leaves are another, but a sandy beach is the best. Bring just enough toys to add interest, but concentrate on imagination. Even if you are not physically able to get in the sand, you can still be a part of the action sitting in a chair. Contribute ideas for construction, praise their work, ask them to bring you a bucket of water and help fill the moat. This is elemental play and grandchildren are never happier than when an adult is really playing with them. By watching the waves come in and slowly take the castle back into the water, both generations can see that some things in life are impermanent, but that doesn't make them any less important or special. We need to learn to enjoy what we are doing in the moment and let it go when its time is done.

A WORD TO THE WISE:

Sunburns are especially dangerous for children because of the increased risk of skin cancer later in life. Pick up sunscreen designed for children over six months with both UVA and UVB protection. SPF 15 is the minimum protection level, but a higher level is better. Apply it thickly and often. The recommendation is 30–45 minutes before going out and every two hours (more if there is a lot of swimming or perspiring). Try to go later in the afternoon so you limit the most intense exposure; UV rays are the worst from around 10 a.m.–4 p.m. Keep in mind that clouds do not eliminate radiation. Eyes can be affected, too, so let the kids be cool and get some shades! If you are using insect repellent, be aware that it can reduce the effectiveness of sunscreen.

AGE OF GRANDCHILD: All

BEST SEASON: Summer

CONTACT: Directory of some Michigan beaches: www.beachtowns.org

Reports on beach quality: www.deq.state.mi.us/beach/

ALSO CHECK OUT:

Holland State Park:
www.michigandnr.com/parksandtrails/Details.aspx?id=458&type=SPRK

Ludington State Park: www.visitludington.com/statepark

Wilderness State Park:
www.michigan.gov/dnr/0,4570,7-153-31154_31260-54042--,00.html

*One way to open your eyes is to ask yourself,
"What if I had never seen this before? What if
I knew I would never see it again?"* RACHEL CARSON

45

Biking

What has wheels, a seat, no motor, and no animals attached, but predates the car in Michigan transportation history? How about a bicycle? This simple contraption has a long and complicated history. The first ones were like scooters, but these were improved on in 1818 by a German, Karl Von Drais. His invention had two wheels and a handlebar, but one thing was missing—the pedals! Those came later, along with a wide variety of other designs and

iterations. The modern safety bicycle, the one we know today, was invented in the 1880s. Of course, we now have road bicycles, cross-trainers, mountain bikes, recumbent bikes, and a variety of other bike styles and shapes, but the important thing is not the purchase—it is the use of the bike.

AARP reflects on the value of biking for grandparents: "Bicycling gives you a low-impact, aerobic workout that strengthens your legs, including your knees. It also can help you lose pounds and stay a healthy weight." Biking is easier on the joints because it is a fluid motion without the compression and pounding that running creates. For children, biking is a way to connect to the outdoors, to gain valuable aerobic exercise, to prevent obesity, and to feel a sense of accomplishment.

Fortunately, we also have bike trails to choose from that are safely removed from cars and other hazards. Like choosing a canoe paddle or a hike, you must consider your fitness, the weather, and the terrain. The terrain might even be the most important—hills are hard and if you are not in shape, they are frustrating. Be sure to check out the options. Here are some excellent Michigan bike trails:

William Field Memorial Hart-Montague Trail State Park

Kal-Haven Trail State Park

Lansing River, Lansing

Mackinac Island—there are no cars allowed on the island

Paint Creek Trail, Rochester

Your ambition needs to match the skill and endurance of your grandchildren. Keep in mind that you are doing this with, and for, them—and if you need more or less pedaling than they do, accommodate that fact. Making the right choice is not complex—take a short ride with younger children and a longer ride with older kids, or, if they have more energy and endurance than you do, try to allow your grandchildren more of a challenge.

Pack a lunch, bring a camera, stop, reflect, and relax. A trail is an adventure if approached right, and not just a connection between starting and stopping. Make it interesting and share your love of a silent sport, the satisfaction of using your own physical power to move, and a speed that allows you to observe and enjoy.

A WORD TO THE WISE:

There are some wonderful options for taking young children on your bike with you. We have an old-fashioned "bugger" (trailer) that fastens to the seat stem and makes a carriage for the child—ours holds two. They look backward as they ride.

Now there are attachable seats that are very similar to the safety seats we use in our cars. They fasten to the handlebars and frame and the child is between your arms and facing forward as you peddle.

A third option is a bike attachment (trailer bikes or tagalongs) that put an extra wheel and seat behind your bike. This is like creating a tandem designed for smaller riders.

AGE OF GRANDCHILD: 3 and up with child carriers, 10 and up for extended rides

BEST SEASON: Spring and fall

CONTACT: William Field Memorial Hart-Montague Trail State Park: www.michigandnr.com/parksandtrails/Details.aspx?id=452&type=SPRK

Kal-Haven Trail State Park: www.michigan.org/property/kal-haven-trail-state-park

Lansing River Trail: http://lansingrivertrail.org/

Mackinac Island: www.mackinacisland.org

Paint Creek Trail: www.paintcreektrail.org

To our children we give two things:
one is roots, the other wings. ANDY ROONEY

46

Botanical Gardens

We were in Detroit on a cold, wet day. It was the end of winter, but not the beginning of spring, and the land looked abused after the snow melted and winter's trash was exposed. What do you do on a day like this? How about going to a botanical garden? Yes, it is great when the plants are up and the landscaping is filled with hummingbirds, bees, and butterflies. We love it when there is a sweet scent in the air, the sky is blue, a light breeze is blowing, and the flowers seem to be radiating an earthly happiness, but it can't always be summer. There are options while we wait.

Don't think only adults wait for spring and summer to arrive. The indoor conservatories within botanical gardens are seasonal oases and they can be that for your grandchildren, too. The Belle Isle Park, an island in the Detroit River, is full of activities and options, and it is a wonderful refuge from the cold rain

and full of inspiring gardens. From the outside, the age and the season make the facility look gloomy—almost gothic— but the sweet aroma of flowers quickly engulfs you. The orchids in bloom will make you forget the weather outside, the water and greenery will bathe the eyes, and the cactus will help dry you out.

In Ann Arbor at the Matthaei Conservatory and Nichols Arboretum, the extensive grounds are beautiful in the sun, but on a rainy day we went inside and saw grandchildren being encouraged to smell the flowers, to observe the unique insect-eating plants, to walk through the misting sprays. In a few steps you can walk into an area of high humidity and then an area of low humidity—a sensation that heightens your appreciation for the different designs and patterns in plants. And when the weather is right, the botanical gardens are great, too; the plants outdoors will attract your attention and provide a healthy setting for your grandchildren to exercise and explore.

Bonding & Bridging

How natural is the connection between children and gardens? Visiting the garden can be an inspiration, and if you do it in the spring, perhaps there will be time for you to plant a garden outside your own home with your grandchildren. Putting seeds in the ground and nurturing a plant, especially a food plant, is a great way to teach the kids about biology, agriculture, and life. It is an exercise in creativity, responsibility and patience. If you want to begin later in the year, grow some indoor plants, let them put in the seeds and get their hands dirty. Buy an indoor grow light and let them measure the growth. You will have a great shared experience that could lead to a lifetime hobby or even a career, but it is also a way to explore the child's health, to talk about vegetables, vitamins, growing strong, and being healthy.

A WORD TO THE WISE:

Education often begins with kindergarten, which means "children's garden" in German. The first kindergarten was opened by Friedrich Froebel in Germany in 1849, but the first U.S. kindergarten began in Watertown, Wisconsin. The first teacher was Margaret Meyer Shurz, whose husband Carl, was the Secretary of the Interior. It began as a German-speaking class and opened in 1856. The concept spread widely, forever linking children, learning, and gardens.

AGE OF GRANDCHILD: Toddler to teenager

BEST SEASON: All

CONTACT: Belle Isle Park; 2 Inselruhe Ave., Detroit, MI 48207; (844) 235-5375; www.michigandnr.com/parksandtrails/Details.aspx?type=SPRK&id=736

Matthaei Botanical Gardens and Nichols Arboretum; (734) 647-7600; www.lsa.umich.edu/mbg/

ALSO CHECK OUT:

Fernwood Botanical Garden and Nature Preserve: www.fernwoodbotanical.org

Frederik Meijer Gardens & Sculpture Park: www.meijergardens.org

W. J. Beal Botanical Garden: www.cpa.msu.edu/beal/

Getting to know the youngest people in my life has been a joy. FRANK TARLOFF

47

Campfire

It may be a primitive connection to our ancient cave-dwelling ancestors, but a campfire is a universal place of sharing and comfort. The Campfire Girls (now Camp Fire USA) explain their name on their website—"First meetings of Camp Fire Girls are held in Vermont [1910]. Dr. Gulick chooses the name 'Camp Fire' because campfires were the origin of the first communities and domestic life. Once people learned to make and control fire, they could develop and nurture a sense of community."

We have enjoyed campfires for many years and have invited people of every age and nationality to our conflagrations, both small and large. So far, we have never found anyone who does not relate to the crackling fire, the smell of the smoke, and the feeling of warmth a fire offers.

Making a fire together helps your grandchildren understand Thoreau's dictum about splitting wood and fire—"they warmed me twice—once while I was splitting them, and again when they were on the fire, so that no fuel could give out more heat." This means you have to teach them what to collect and what to leave behind.

Teach your grandchildren that a good fire is made of wood that is dry and not bigger than the size of their wrist. Engage the children in building and lighting the fire and let them learn to minimize our impact while enjoying this very natural pleasure. A good fire is not so large that you have to sit a long way off to avoid the heat, you want it to be just the right size to light up your spot on Earth, but big enough to provide heat needed for warmth or cooking, if you want to add s'mores and other campfire food to the get-together.

Campfires are perfect for stories and conversation. Around the fire we lose perspective of who is speaking, which means that age, sex, and all the other characteristics that separate us fall to the wayside. We all become equals and it becomes a place to share and listen to one another. Like fireworks in miniature, the sparks dance in the darkness. The flames are mesmerizing and we become the source of ideas, images, and thoughts, instead of relying on radio, TV, or video.

Bonding & *Bridging* ∞∞∞∞∞∞∞∞∞∞∞∞∞∞∞∞∞∞∞∞∞∞∞∞∞∞∞∞∞

Night is very long in the north. Grandparents can use the campfire to bridge this barrier. A fire seems safe because it provides light and warmth. We can cook on the fire and we can use it as a means to communicate. These are strong bonding activities. In some ways the circle of light is like an invisible tent that encompasses everyone around it. In this way, use the campfire to help your grandchildren fight night terrors and fears. Have them face away from the fire, give them time to let their eyes adjust, and then have them tell you what they see. Have them lie back and adjust to the sky and the wonderful universe around them. If you are lucky you will hear sounds in the night and you can soothe them with the knowledge that these are not threatening sounds, just the noise made by life in the dark. Finally, you can help them understand that the fire that gives you all the comfort for this wonderful evening, is, in fact, dangerous in its own right.

A WORD TO THE WISE:

Remember to place an emphasis on food. Food on a stick allows grandchildren to cook and eat and concentrate on the positives. The old recipe for s'mores has been a staple for years: a cooked marshmallow squashed between two graham crackers with a little wedge of chocolate in between. In fact, the Campfire Girls were founded not far from the Hershey factory, and s'mores seem like a natural development.

AGE OF GRANDCHILD: 3 and up

BEST SEASON: Summer and fall, but we also like equinox and solstice fires.

ALSO CHECK OUT:

Campfire Cooking: http://eartheasy.com/play_campfire_cooking.htm

Funny Campfire Stories: www.ultimatecampresource.com/site/camp-activities/funny-campfire-stories.page-1.html

Hiawatha National Forest: www.fs.usda.gov/hiawatha

Huron-Manistee National Forests: www.fs.usda.gov/hmnf

Michigan State Parks: www.michigandnr.com/parksandtrails/

Ottawa National Forest: www.fs.usda.gov/ottawa/

My grandfather was a giant of a man . . . When he walked, the earth shook.
When he laughed, the birds fell out of the trees. His hair caught fire
from the sun. His eyes were patches of sky. Eth Clifford, The Remembering Box

48

Canoeing

While we picture big ships on the Great Lakes and fishing boats on the inland waters, the canoe was the first vessel to really travel and explore the state. The birchbark canoe was the first truly revolutionary transportation invention in Michigan and its successors in aluminum, fiberglass, and Kevlar continue to be a wonderful and intimate way to see wild places. Today, the Manistee

and Au Sable rivers are wonderful, wild and scenic options for exploring natural and secluded waterways. While it is still a great way to relax, learn, and get healthy exercise, it is something that requires some skill, so don't take your grandchild out if you have not canoed before. Too many first-time paddlers go swimming unintentionally, and that is not how you want to have your grandchild learn about this marvelous outdoor sport.

The Sylvania Wilderness in the U.P. offers outstanding lakes and wilderness to explore, but streams have a completely different feeling. The movement of a stream constantly propels you to new discoveries, even when you stop paddling. The scenery, and therefore the opportunities, are constant, with each bend in the constantly twisting river providing a new setting.

The Manistee starts as a small stream near Grayling and flows 200 miles with few rapids and no portages, making it a truly magnificent place to explore. Like all rivers, it grows as it flows, with each tributary creek and river adding to the volume of water. This means a change in the plants, the shoreline animals, and the fish, and it's easy to add a pole to your equipment list. The upper area is a quicker float, but the lower and wider (100 feet) sections have the best swimming holes.

The 135-mile Au Sable River also starts near Grayling; the combined Manistee and Au Sable river valleys neatly cut across the state from Lake Michigan to Lake Huron. For many people this is Michigan's river, the river of story, legend, as well as clear water, sandy campsites, and tradition. A wonderful river to explore, it does have some fast water, so read the guides and choose the best sections that fit your skills. If you feel up to it, a campout on a river trip is one of those very special opportunities to really share and bond. A canoe allows you to bring much more than you might if you were backpacking, and it lets you access remote sites. There, the quiet movement of the water becomes the background as you rest in camp in front of a campfire.

Bonding & Bridging

In an age when everything has a motor on it, makes noise, and goes fast, we expect that the grandparent will go a little slower. A grandparent can help a child understand that slowing down means experiencing more. We paddle not to get somewhere, but to be somewhere. A motor removes the fresh scent of river air, the sound of subtle things like swaying trees brushing branches against one another, or small birds calling out their territories. Rivers are big ideas, wild concepts, big systems, but they invite us to float and become one with their energies. Far from slowing down, canoeing is, in fact, about going farther and further to connect with nature and land.

A WORD TO THE WISE:

You might not think of a river as a lesson in physics, but you better understand a few principles so hazards are minimized. You can teach some science lessons as well. Because a stream flows, it goes downstream—literally down in gradient—so upstream is always going toward the source. Water flows in a straight line. It does not curve even though the streambed does. So it flows to the outside of a corner with the most power, making the outside of the curve both the deepest and the most likely to have downed trees. When you want to steer, you must be moving faster or slower than the current or you have no control. When you see an obstacle, you must move well in advance. Finally, remember a canoe is like a lever and since the stern paddler is closer to the end than the bow paddler, the person in the back will overpower the front and one must adjust their stroke to compensate for this.

AGE OF GRANDCHILD: 10 and up

BEST SEASON: Summer

CONTACT: Big Manistee River:
www.visitmanisteecounty.com/outdoor-manistee-county/water-adventure

Michigan Natural Rivers Program: www.michigan.gov/dnr/0,4570,7-153-10364_52259_31442-95823--,00.html

ALSO CHECK OUT:

Huron River Water Trail:
www.michigan.org/property/huron-river-water-trail/

Pere Marquette River: www.rivers.gov/rivers/pere-marquette.php

The closest friends I have made all through life have been people who also grew up close to a loved and living grandmother or grandfather. MARGARET MEAD

49

Cemetery Visit

Grandparents can share some lessons better than anyone else. For this reason we suggest a visit to a cemetery, even though this hardly seems like a typical outing. For our grandchildren, our death will probably be the first great loss in their lives. I know that this is as hard to read as it is to write, but having lost a 21-year-old son in New Zealand, I also know that the weight of death is excruciatingly difficult. It is not necessary for us to have a "when I die" talk with our grandchildren, but we should let death be a fact and part of our life. This will make it easier. Some of you may think that religion will take care of this, but it won't. Loss is personal, not religious, even though religion can help ease the pain.

Cemeteries hold many lessons, and it can be a good experience for you to be the one who helps your grandchild learn about this topic. We recommend choosing old cemeteries, ones that reflect history and events. We recommend the Swedish cemetery in Cheboygan, which reflects the ethnic history of the region.

Look at the monuments, but look closely at the gravestones. If you are in a very old cemetery, you will find many headstones from particular periods that commemorate children who died because of diphtheria, smallpox, or any other

number of diseases. These are lessons in good health, good hygiene, and good medicine. It may comfort your grand-children to know that preventive medicines and shots help protect them from such tragic epidemics.

For a good pioneer cemetery, check out Holt Cemetery located in Morley, on Aurelius Road about a block north of Cedar Street. This cemetery opened in 1853 and covers 1.1 acres. It has been declared an Ingham County historic site and is included in the Michigan State Register of Historic Sites. Another pioneer cemetery is found just outside Detroit in Southfield, where the United Presbyterian Church Cemetery began in 1832. Most graves here date to the nineteenth century, and they include Isaac Heth, one of the area's first settlers.

We tend to think that cemeteries last forever, but do they? One of the earliest cemeteries we have is the Norton Mound Group near Grand Rapids, an American Indian burial site, but where are the other burial locations for the native peoples of the state?

Bonding & Bridging ⋈⋈⋈⋈⋈⋈⋈⋈⋈⋈⋈⋈⋈⋈

If you visit cemeteries where people you knew are buried, you can tell their stories. Even after our deaths, we live on in photos, stories, and the memories of our loved ones. This is why we should tell our family's story. Many societies without writing did this for centuries and passed down stories from generation to generation. Now that we have books and writing, sometimes people forget about these stories and the spoken word, but how many families have books written about their experiences?

If you have created a family tree, this is a good time to share it. As strange as it sounds, a cemetery is where a family tree comes alive. It's good to talk about where you came from and help your grandchildren think about who their ancestors were. What is an ancestor? This is where your discussions begin.

A WORD TO THE WISE:

Bring a large piece of paper, a crayon, chalk, or charcoal. Place the paper over the old gravestones and put the chalk or charcoal on its side. Then rub it over the paper against the gravestone. The words and images should transfer without doing any damage to the gravestone. This can be taken home, a unique art project and a tool for recalling what you saw.

AGE OF GRANDCHILD: 10 and up

BEST SEASON: Any

ALSO CHECK OUT:

Assumption Grotto: http://nighttraintodetroit.com/2013/08/05/every-cemetery-in-detroit-assumption-grotto/

Historic Elmwood Cemetery & Foundation: www.elmwoodhistoriccemetery.org/

Michigan Historical Cemeteries: http://michigan.hometownlocator.com/features/historical,class,cemetery.cfm

Mt. Elliott Cemetery: www.mtelliott.com/mtelliott/

Norton Mound Group: www.michigan.gov/som/0,4669,7-192-29938_68915-54607--,00.html

Silverbrook Cemetery: www.ci.niles.mi.us/DeptsAndServices/DPW/SilverbrookCemetery.htm

Grandchildren are the dots that connect the lines from generation to generation. Lois Wyse

50

Children's Museums

Is this a museum or a playground? Does it matter? To the kids there is no question about what the museum is—it is their place. There are multiple floors of creativity. Color, design, and educational content are interwoven into one of the most child-engaging places possible. It is the job of the grandparent to guide them through, letting the children's imagination make the choices while you watch over safety and the possible conflict that can arise from lots of little hands and feet concentrating on the objects that have grabbed their attention.

This is creative play, and imagination is the real tool at work here—it leads to creative thinking and effective problem solving later in life. The grandparent needs to play along and let the grandchildren (and their imaginations) take over. Don't worry if they get wet in the water areas—bring extra clothing. Sometimes it is necessary to cajole and make sure that all of the children are sharing, but don't turn into a bully even on behalf of your grandchildren. Let the children learn how to play together and enjoy the fantastic worlds constructed by each display.

Michigan has some exceptional children's museums, from the Discovery Center in Marquette and the Curious Kids' Museum in St. Joseph to the Children's Museum in Detroit. There is a museum near you throughout the state; take advantage of all of them as you travel.

Think about the way children try to emulate adults. Here, they are encouraged to act out the roles they have created in their minds. They are offered adult settings but not told how to fulfill the roles they choose. Whether it is a dairy farm, a market, or a TV studio—the story is theirs to create. As the supervising adult, allow them this freedom and do not impose your ideas—instead, observe, enjoy, and learn.

Museums see the role of grandparents as essential to the child and many offer a season pass at the parents' rate. These passes often are accepted at other children's museums as well. It is a very good deal!

Bonding & Bridging ◇◇

In play, the child also looks for approval, and grandparents are ideal candidates to encourage, praise, and offer new insights. It is important for grandparents to allow the children to have the experience—that means stepping back and letting the child explore. It means not reaching in and competing with children for the balls and boats and materials—but rather, letting the grandchildren know how to get these things for themselves.

Use the reading area and the lunch breaks and the ride home to talk to the children about what they liked. Help them learn to pace themselves and process the experience. "How did that . . . work?" "What did you like best and why?"

A WORD TO THE WISE:

This is your day to enable and observe. Take advantage of programs where the staff helps children use art to focus their energy and enthusiasm. And when it feels overwhelming, let the children know that Grandpa or Grandma is a little tired and if they go to a quieter museum area, they can stay even longer.

AGE OF GRANDCHILD: Up to age 10 seems perfect.

BEST SEASON: All

CONTACT: Ann Arbor Hands-On Museum: 220 E Ann St., Ann Arbor, MI 48104; (734) 995-5439; www.aahom.org

Curious Kids' Museum: 415 Lake Blvd., St. Joseph, MI 49085; (269) 983-2543; www.curiouskidsmuseum.org

Detroit Children's Museum: 6134 Second Ave., Detroit, MI 48202; (313) 873-8100; http://detroitk12.org/childrens_museum/

Flint Children's Museum: 1602 W Third Ave., Flint, MI 48504; (810) 767-5437; www.thefcm.org

Grand Rapids Children's Museum: 11 Sheldon Ave. NE, Grand Rapids, MI 49503; (616) 235-4726; www.grcm.org

Great Lakes Children's Museum: 13240 S West Bayshore Dr. (M-22), Traverse City, MI 49685; (231) 932-4526; www.greatlakeskids.org

Upper Peninsula Children's Museum: 123 W Baraga Ave., Marquette, MI 49855; (906) 226-3911; www.upchildrensmuseum.org/

*Grandparents and grandchildren
are God's gift to each other.* Unknown

51

Cooking Together

"Food comes from the grocery store." This is a common belief among a large portion of urban children who do not see farms regularly, who do not hunt, fish, or even cook! As grandparents, we have the opportunity to turn the kitchen into a science center. All types of cooking require reading (recipes), math (measuring), and science (the interaction of compounds), so set aside the time, jump in, and start your grandchild on a new path.

Cooking with your grandchildren adds all sorts of positive memories and depending upon their age, they can help in any number of ways. You can let them use a cookie cutter and decorate your creations, or they can take part in measuring, mixing, baking, and, of course, eating.

Be prepared to do the majority of the work. If they get bored and wander off, don't force them to come back; they'll come back for the tasting. Be patient and let them get intrigued. Success comes from following some simple rules.

First, choose a recipe that your grand-child will like. This should generally be a simple recipe (unless you're working with an older grandchild). Then, put an apron on everyone (we know that aprons are getting harder to find) and have everyone wash their hands. Good hygiene is an important lesson, and while cleanliness might be tough to achieve, keep it in mind.

Set out the ingredients. When you invite them to cook with you, the last thing you want to do is make them wait while you sort out your cupboards. Set up stations that keep the children away from sharp knifes and hot pans. There will be three stations—one for mixing ingredients, the oven or stove for cooking them, and another spot for decorating or serving the results. Have a stool, if necessary, so that they don't have to stretch to reach the countertop. Help them measure, but do it over a separate bowl so that extra ingredients do not fall into your final product.

For younger children, decorating is the most fun, although sampling is always very popular. In fact, dough may start disappearing before it gets to the oven. How can you beat an activity that is tactile, smells great, looks good, and tastes great?

Bonding & Bridging

In our research we came upon a significant statement—"Build kids, not cookies." What a great perspective! Cooking is all about sharing and creating. Don't even think of cooking together unless you are going to invest the time. Don't rush, don't call on the phone; this is no time for multitasking, but a time for concentration.

When the final products are done, especially baked goods, children can learn the lesson of delayed gratification while they wait for their creation to cool before eating. Think of some things you can do during this time—like cleaning up the area and dishes you used. Explain that cooking takes patience; it takes time for fruit to ripen or time to prepare and cook barbecue. You might work by setting the table or by creating a fun drink while you wait.

A WORD TO THE WISE:

Making playdough is a good way to introduce young children to cooking. All you need is 7–8 cups of flour, 3 cups of salt, 3 tablespoons of cream of tartar, ¼ cup of vegetable oil, 4 cups of hot water, and some food coloring. Mix the first three; add oil and water and knead. Break up the dough into smaller units so you can make different colors when you knead. While they can't eat playdough, making it teaches them many steps involved in cooking, and all ages can contribute. Two-year-olds can scrub and tear, three-year-olds can mix and pour, and four- and five-year-olds can learn to measure.

AGE OF GRANDCHILD: 3 and up

BEST SEASON: Winter

ALSO CHECK OUT:

Cooking Classes in Detroit: www.metroparent.com/daily/food/cooking-with-kids/cooking-classes-in-metro-detroit-southeast-michigan/

Cooking with Kids: www.childrensrecipes.com/

Recipes to Cook with Kids: www.parenting.com/gallery/recipes-cook-kids

The Science of Cooking: www.exploratorium.edu/cooking/

Grandparents, like heroes, are as necessary to a child's growth as vitamins. JOYCE ALLSTON

52

Drive-In Restaurants

In the 1950s and '60s, the drive-in was the closest thing to today's fast-food restaurants. They share some similarities; they are convenient and designed for the traveler and the car, but the comparison stops there. Drive-ins were not fast-food or simple "burgers and fries" menus, but freshly cooked food for each order. The first drive-ins opened in 1936 in Glendale, California, and they reached their peak popularity in the 1950s.

It was Detroit's cars of the 1950s that helped popularize the drive-in and made people want to get out and be seen in their cars. The drive-in was a place for luxuriating in your car or sitting at an outside table with your car in view. People talked to people in the next car, met friends, and spent time. Fast food—forget it, when I was in high school we spent the entire evening at the drive-in.

After World War II, drive-ins added canopies to provide shade and shelter from the weather. Carhops served your meals by foot or on roller skates. Ever since, drive-ins have continued to provide the unique curbside service that makes them so different from a fast-food joint. You are expected to spend a little time here, to relax from the road.

Today, Michigan is lucky to have a number of drive-in options to compete with the overwhelming fast-food franchises. For example, there is Nip and Sip in Lansing, Clyde's Drive-In in Sault Ste. Marie, and Allen's Root Beer Drive-In in Coldwater. Luckily, you can still experience the taste, the smell, and the feeling of the drive-in with your grandchild. For them it must seem like ancient history.

Bonding & Bridging

With fast food so ingrained in today's society that some schools even allow fast-food restaurants to serve lunch, the concept of driving in and slowing down is something the kids will not have experienced, unless they are lucky enough to live near a drive-in. How fun for you to take the kids and order from the car—put some '50s music on the radio, or in the CD or tape player.

Tell the kids how this was part of travel and our social experience. Sip that big mug of root beer and talk about how things are different. Compare fast food to the drive-in. It might be fun to play a tape of an old radio program or something else that you might have enjoyed, and if you want to connect even more, select an old *Happy Days* video and share with the kids when you get home.

A WORD TO THE WISE:

A&W began in 1919 in Lodi, California, as a root beer created by Roy Allen, who bought the formula from an Arizona pharmacist. The blend of barks, berries, and herbs has remained a guarded secret ever since. Roy opened a stand to sell his root beer, and the creamy liquid flew off the shelf. Allen's business partner was an employee named Wright, and the name was settled: A&W. When the drive-in craze hit, A&W used it to expand nationwide and over 2,000 root beer stands covered the country.

AGE OF GRANDCHILD: All

BEST SEASON: Summer

CONTACT: A&W Locations: www.awrestaurants.com/locations

Diners, Drive-Ins & Dives, Michigan:
www.dinersdriveinsdiveslocations.com/michigan-locations.html

Michigan Roadside Architecture: www.roadarch.com/eateries/midi.html

The Best of Michigan, Past and Present:
www.waterwinterwonderland.com/restaurants.aspx

Perfect love sometimes does not come until grandchildren are born. Welsh Proverb

53

Ethnic Celebrations

As grandparents, it is likely we are only two, three, or four generations removed from those who immigrated to the United States. Most European immigrants came in the 1800s and early 1900s, and tragically, many people of African descent arrived against their will over 100 years ago. More recently, immigrants have arrived from Asia, Africa, and Central America. All of these people and all of these cultures have been thrown together into what is often called a "melting pot," but which I consider more of a "stew pot," because while we all are in the same country, living next to one another, together we create a delicious dish of traditions and beliefs, but we retain our identity.

We are like bits of carrots, and potatoes, and onions—unique in flavor and appearance and proud of our places of origin.

In Europe, people find it strange that we Americans identify or think of ourselves as hyphenated people: Irish-American, African-American, Italian-American, and on and on. But they are a people whose families have lived in the same country, often the same village, and sometimes even the same house, for centuries. They do not know the meaning of leaving the place where their roots go deep and settling in a totally new land. The custom of identifying ourselves with the old countries is something that will fade with time as each new generation becomes further removed from that distant homeland and as our grandchildren marry and intermix with others of multiple nationalities. We truly will become a sort of Heinz 57 citizenry, a beautiful blending of skin tones and accents and customs.

But for those of us who grew up with the traditions, music, and stories of the lands left behind, there is a desire to share that history with our grandchildren. The many ethnic festivals held throughout the year give us that opportunity. Even if you can't find a festival that matches your own specific nationality, take your grandchildren to these festivals and expose them to the world without leaving the country, or even the city.

Bonding & Bridging

There are many ways that grandparents and grandchildren can enjoy ethnic festivals. If the ethnicity is part of your heritage, you can explore it and its influence on your family today. Why did your family travel from another place? What did they come to do? Why did they choose the place you live? Are there foods you eat that are part of your heritage? At an ethnic festival you can introduce your grandchild to foods they might not otherwise taste. They might bring back memories for you as you remember the smells and flavors. Ethnic festivals that do not represent your ancestry can still challenge the children to experience new tastes, and help them understand other people and help them to appreciate diversity. Listen to the music, look at the costumes, and enjoy the parades. Bring along a map, participate, and take an inexpensive journey to another land.

A WORD TO THE WISE:

For me, the highlight is always dancing. Almost every culture has its own unique folk dance, and children will relish the chance to dance with you and the other grown-ups. They may not be able to get the steps right, but skipping and hopping are always acceptable. If there is swinging involved, that's even better. When my two children were seven and eight years old, I took them to an Irish dance, called a "ceili." We laughed and danced until we were out of breath. We kept going as they grew older, and I even managed to get them to attend as teenagers (luckily, my son had a girlfriend who enjoyed going). Today, as adults, they still enjoy going, and I expect we will introduce their children to ceilis in the future.

AGE OF GRANDCHILD: Any age, but best if they can walk.

BEST SEASON: Anytime the festival is held—often in conjunction with holidays and feast days of ethnic origin.

ALSO CHECK OUT:

African World Festival, Detroit: August

Bavarian Festival, Frankenmuth: June, www.bavarianfestival.org

Greek Festival, Saginaw: June, (989) 793-8822

Heikinpaiva Finnish Festival, Hancock: January, http://pasty.com/heikki

Irish Festival, Clare: March, www.clareirishfestival.com

Polish Festival, Bronson: July, www.bronson-mi.com/about/polish-festival

Grandmas never run out of hugs or cookies. UNKNOWN

54

Farmers Markets

I was lucky to have a grandmother who had been a farmer. When she moved to the city, a weekly trip to the farmers market was her way to keep her past alive. Many Saturday mornings I was roused from bed at dawn to accompany my mother and grandmother to the market. Any grumpiness I felt at this

intrusion faded as soon as I smelled the ripe cantaloupe. The memories of those Saturday mornings with her and the sensuous smells of the Earth's bounty are some of the best I have.

There are four main ways to connect children to food and make such memories: (1) spend time on a farm; (2) plant and maintain a garden; (3) get your fruits from vendors who let you pick them yourself; or (4) visit the farmers markets that exist all over Michigan. Farmers markets are not just roadside stands; they are organized efforts to bring local producers in contact with consumers. Here is a place where you can introduce your grandchildren to the people who grow food. Here they can see seasonal, locally grown foods and learn about the beauty and richness of agriculture and how it provides for the basic needs in each of us.

In today's world, very few children have the experience of caring for animals, picking food for the evening meal, or even running free in a pasture. A farmers market, with its colorful tables of produce, flowers, meats, and baked goods may be as close as many children will get to being at a farm, or meeting a farmer. Go early and wander leisurely. Sometimes there are samples to nibble, and there is always great people-watching. The smells, sounds, textures, and colors are images that will stay with your grandchild—just as these images have stayed with me.

There are so many lessons in this visit. Think about all of the contrasts between a farmers market and a supermarket, such as the packaging (or lack thereof). Also consider what healthy food is and what the word "organic" means. At the farmers market you can ask these questions of the vendors selling their vegetables and fruits. They may not be able to answer all your questions, but they can fill in a lot of the unknowns about the foods we eat.

Bonding & Bridging

It's easy to take food for granted. Whenever we want it, we know where to get it. A simple trip to the grocery store takes care of our needs. Rarely do we consider the question: "Where does this food come from?"

A farmers market is a chance to open your grandchildren's eyes to the hard work and dedication that goes into everything we eat. They can meet some of the people who work tirelessly to provide us with food. Tell them how important farmers are to our way of life. Share with them how difficult growing crops truly is and how we would struggle if there were no farmers to do this job. For older children, you may also want to bring up third-world countries in which food supplies are scarce. Either way, this is definitely a time when you want to help your grandchildren learn to appreciate every meal.

A WORD TO THE WISE:

Ask your grandchildren to think about what they'd like to have for lunch, and then spend your visit finding the best ingredients—it can become a treasure hunt. Even the pickiest eater probably likes tomatoes, corn on the cob, or watermelon. To complete the morning's excursion, let them choose a bouquet of freshly cut flowers to put on the table during your meal. Then engage them by preparing the meal at home or on a picnic. Let them see the second half of the food circle—where the food goes into the kitchen and is prepared for our consumption. If this is exciting, it may also circumvent the natural pickiness that seems to infect so many children.

AGE OF GRANDCHILD: All

BEST SEASON: Late spring, summer and early fall

CONTACT: Michigan Farm Direct Locations:
www.farmerdirect2you.com/farms-MI.aspx

Michigan Farmers Market Association: http://mifma.org/

Michigan Pick Your Own: www.pickyourown.org/MI.htm

I like to do nice things for my grandchildren—like buy them those toys I've always wanted to play with. GENE PERRET

55

Farm Life

We are always looking for farms where you can take your grandchildren. When Kate and I grew up, many of our relatives lived on farms, and it was easy to go for a tractor ride, feed the chickens, milk the cows, and explore the hayloft. But those days are gone for many of our children and that is a shame for many reasons.

A farm is the best place for beginning to understand biology. Here one finds a connection with living animals, animals that are not confined by cages, but are rather a part of the landscape, as well as the life of the farm family.

Today's factory farms, corporate feed lots, and packaged foods disguise our connection with other forms of life. They sanitize what we eat and substitute names like pork for pig and beef for cow. Things come wrapped, uniform, and sterilized.

The vegetables look perfect, which in and of itself should raise questions. So how do we connect our grandchildren with the heritage of farming, with our gardens, with the animals we raise and why we raise them? Go to a farm.

As more and more of the population lives in the city and suburbs, we find both the number of farms and farmers dropping. So we need to go to Wellington Farm Park, near Grayling, or Domino Farm, just outside of Ann Arbor.

Each of these locations gives you a different perspective on farm life. Wellington Farm combines history and farming. At the farm it is always 1932, a point in the Great Depression when farmers worked to feed their families and earn a few extra dollars, but they could not afford all the mechanized and chemical additions that would come in postwar farm life. These were true dirt farmers who did whatever they had to for survival. Not only do costumed volunteers help bring the Wellington Farm history to life, but the historic buildings are used in the farming that they carry out today.

At Domino Farms you are in the modern era with an emphasis on animals that can be fed and petted. Hayrides, pony rides, and lots of different corrals and animals attract people to this location for birthdays and visits.

A farm visit can be the starting point for many shared adventures. Now that your grandchild knows where food comes from, they can participate in shopping, cooking, and gardening. You can go back to the farm in different seasons and help them explore the changes that relate to time and growth.

A farmers market visit will be a wonderful follow-up. The color and feeling that you get walking around the colorful fruits and vegetables, the variety of sizes and shapes and the touch and smells that are part of the market provide another way to touch the Earth and share its bounty. In an era when fast food often means "fast fat" and we are concerned about obesity and health, the farm is a good place to get grounded in good nutrition and healthful living.

A WORD TO THE WISE:

If your grandchildren really enjoy the farm, Wellington Farm offers an opportunity for you to camp on the grounds and spend a week actually working on the farm. You can drive a tractor, feed the animals, haul hay, split wood, and do all the things that were part of the visits we used to make to our aunts and uncles. This is exercise with a purpose that includes fresh air and even has opportunities for picnics and canoe trips. You can gather with a farm community of campers, share recipes, toss horseshoes, tell stories, and maybe work together to create the kind of meals that farms are famous for.

AGE OF GRANDCHILD: 3 to 12

BEST SEASON: Summer

CONTACT: Wellington Farm, 6944 S Military Rd., Grayling, MI 49738; (989) 348-5187; www.wellingtonfarmpark.org

The Petting Farm at Domino's Farms, 3001 Earhart Rd., Ann Arbor, MI 48105; (734) 998-0182; www.pettingfarm.com

ALSO CHECK OUT:

Discover Michigan Farm Fun:
www.michiganfarmfun.com/collection.asp?ait=cv&cid=3

Lewis Farm Market & Petting Farm: www.lewisfarmmarket.com

Michigan Pick Your Own: www.pickyourown.org/MI.htm

Bringing up a family should be an adventure, not an anxious discipline in which everybody is constantly graded for performance. **Milton R. Saperstein**

56

Ferry Across Lake Michigan

Lake Michigan forms one border of the state, but it is also something of a roadblock. Traveling to Wisconsin means traveling around the lake, and that takes a lot of time, (especially if you have to go through Chicago). But there is another option. Besides sunbathing, swimming, tossing pebbles in the surf, watching storms, and fishing—you could just hop on a ferry and go across the lake.

We do not have a culture of cruise boats in the Great Lakes, but we have a wonderful history of working boats. Your grandchildren have heard about pirates, explorers, and sailors. They know the romance of the sea from film and story, so how about giving them a little sea time yourself?

The Lake Express Carferry from Muskegon to Milwaukee is only two and a half hours long each way. It is a modern high-speed ferry with seats inside and out. A longer option (four hours) is the historic SS *Badger*, which connects Ludington, Michigan, and Manitowoc, Wisconsin.

To enjoy your cruise, think about how this adventure feels for your grandchild. They will be excited by the boat and the water. They will want to explore the boat when you first get on and watch as it pulls away from the dock. Point out the gulls and the shoreline. Help them find things to focus on. Then as the ship moves out of port, be ready for relaxation—isn't that what a cruise is for?

Bring some food or buy some from the on-board cafeteria. Have a book to read, and maybe bring a puzzle, a board game, and binoculars. The SS *Badger* has a movie theater, and this is not a bad option for part of the trip because the round trip will be eight hours of boat time. They also have a kids' port play area for younger children. Enjoy both the voyage and the contrast between the port cities.

Bring your car if you want a longer stay or want to make a round trip that includes both ferries, but it is not necessary if you are just looking for a boat ride. Bring bikes for a cheaper and healthier option to cars.

Bonding & Bridging

Time spent on the ferry is good for reading, resting, and playing, but it is also time for personal sharing. Enjoy the moments to get your memory refreshed. Ask your grandchildren what makes them feel good. What makes them happy? If they are old enough, talk about what makes them feel relaxed.

Americans sometimes lose track of the value of relaxation. We are so driven in our work, studies, and even our play that we lose this important need. Hinduism and Buddhism have significant rituals and beliefs that center on the ability to relax and meditate. For others, relaxation accompanies laughter. Ask your grandchildren what makes them laugh, what makes them smile.

A WORD TO THE WISE:

Sea sickness can destroy a wonderful experience. Here are ways to avoid a bad voyage. First, ask your doctor before taking any medicines and make sure you eat before your ride, but stay away from acidic and greasy foods. A candy bar is OK, but don't overdo the sweets; saltine crackers work well for motion because they absorb acidity. Water, milk, cranberry juice, and apple juice are better than orange juice and most carbonated drinks; however, the phosphoric acid in Coke and Pepsi is said to help if you're feeling queasy. If you're worried about sea sickness, stay on deck and watch the horizon, as this can help prevent dizziness.

AGE OF GRANDCHILD: 4 to 12

BEST SEASON: Summer

CONTACT: Lake Express: (866) 914-1010; www.lake-express.com; SS Badger: (800) 841-4243; www.ssbadger.com

ALSO CHECK OUT:

Ferry to Bois Blanc Island from Cheboygan: www.bbiferry.com

Ironton Ferry from Charlevoix: www.michigan.org/property/ironton-ferry-lake-charlevoix

Shepler's Mackinac Island Ferry: www.sheplersferry.com

Star Line: www.mackinacisland.net/ferries

Even now, I am not old. I never think of it, and yet I am a grandmother to eleven grandchildren. GRANDMA MOSES

57

Fireworks

There is something about watching fireworks that is hard to replicate in other shared adventures with your grandchildren. Maybe watching fireworks is unique because you are actually telling them to stay up late, you are taking them out into the dark, and you are going to watch a colorful, loud, and unusual display—one that would be illegal if you tried it yourself.

One listing of fireworks in Michigan has over 525 events on the calendar for the year! The Chinese may have invented fireworks, but the big displays that celebrate our nation's birthday have made us the "fireworks for fun" leader. There are many places to view Lake Michigan, but it is hard to beat the Bay City Fireworks Festival—four days of celebration with music, food, carnival, crafts, and festivities. When it gets dark, the fireworks begin along the Saginaw River. Find a seat, spread a blanket, and watch the show and the reflections! The fireworks are set off all three nights of the festival so you should be able to find the right night for you and the grandchildren to take this in.

If you can't make it to Bay City, you can join Battle Creek's air show and celebration. All of these celebrations include lots of activities to fill the daylight hours, as well as the displays after dark.

Fourth of July celebrations are not limited to large cities. Small-town fireworks reinforce the true meaning of our national celebration. Imagine being on Mackinac Island with bunting hanging from the railings, the fort filled with historical characters, music in the parks, and a grand picnic before the fireworks. Or you can enjoy a fountain and fireworks in Grand Haven where they coordinate both water displays and pyrotechnics! Holland, with its gardens and ethnic displays, gives one a different feeling altogether.

This is also a perfect opportunity for grandparents to help children overcome the fear of the dark. Imagine it: a perfect summer evening, a blanket spread on the grass of the park, or near the lake, a pillow under your head, and if you're lucky, the stars shine through and you can point out simple waypoints like the Big Dipper and the North Star to tide them over until the fireworks start and they "ooh" and "aah" along with you.

Bonding & Bridging

Fireworks hold a fascinating place in our American psyche. They are a physical display of light and sound, as well as a symbol. Discuss the connection between the Fourth of July and our national anthem. What is it that makes the fireworks so much a part of our nation's most important holiday? What is the connection between the lyrics of our national anthem and the most audacious part of our annual celebration? Here is a chance to talk about symbols, patriotism, and celebration. This is a story that will take time to understand, but observing the fireworks is an opportunity for awe and to delve into deeper meaning.

A WORD TO THE WISE:

Remember that children are not used to being up this late, and they do not know how dangerous fireworks can be. This is a chance to give them safety tips in a positive environment. As they grow older, the fascination with fireworks and gunpowder will change. How you handle this with them when they are young could be important for their future. Consult the website we have listed regarding what is legal in the state. If you break the law, you are also setting an example.

AGE OF GRANDCHILD: 3 and up

BEST SEASON: Summer; July 4 is the biggest day.

CONTACT: Battle Creek Field of Flight Air Show & Balloon Festival: www.bcballoons.com

Bay City Fireworks Festival: http://baycityfireworksfestival.com

Michigan Fireworks Displays: www.michiganfireworks.com

ALSO CHECK OUT:

A List of Legal Fireworks in Michigan: www.michigan.gov/documents/lara/fireworks_381040_7.pdf

Grand Haven Coast Guard Festival: www.coastguardfest.org

Michigan Events: www.michigan.org

There is no grandfather who does not adore his grandson. Victor Hugo

58

Fishing

A translucent line, a hook, a sinker, a worm, and a pole: these are ingredients that could change a life. Fishing is one of the most basic sports in the world and also one of the most popular. If there is water around, fishing is part of the scene. Of course, it is a multi-billion-dollar industry, but fun doesn't have to do with how much you spent, but what you caught. A sunny nibbling at the bait is a terrible tease, just as a small bass is an explosion of energy and excitement.

Grandparents need to keep the activity simple. You do not need boats and engines, a depth finder, or a tackle box that you need a block and tackle to lift. Just get the basics and take your grandchild to the lake or the river. It is all about excitement and anticipation, maybe even magic. Drop a worm in, pull a fish out.

Start with panfish. They are simple, abundant in the right places, and your grandchild can experience success in a hurry. If you make them work for the big one, you are likely to see the excitement replaced with boredom. Concentrate the first fishing trip on their excitement, not the record lunker.

Try for a bluegill, which one fishing expert says is ounce for ounce, the toughest fighting fish on the planet. They are enthusiastic feeders, so all you have to do is locate them and they will be waiting in line to get on your hook. Spawning beds are in shallow water near reeds. The best rig is a test line that can hold 4–6 pounds, with a bobber 15–18 inches above a small hook that's baited with a bit of worm.

You will have to fight the temptation to grab the line and say, "Let me show you." Does it matter if one gets away? Be patient. Isn't that one of fishing's lessons? Enjoy the setting and the excitement, and then, when you are done catching fish, enjoy the bounty of your catch.

Bonding & Bridging

Catch-and-release is a wonderful idea to teach children when they are young. This very simple idea encompasses sportsmanship and conservation, and children need to understand these early. The idea is: catching is the enjoyment, and there is no enjoyment if we harvest too much. We need to let the fish grow, reproduce, and keep the lake stocked. The idea of taking the limit can be an exercise in greed.

Talk about greed, about conservation, about limited resources, and making choices about what we need and what we want. These ideas are hard to cover in normal conversation, but when you are having fun catching bluegills and have to decide when it's time to put them back, you have a perfect setting.

A WORD TO THE WISE:

This is not about records; it is about fun. Keep everything simple: the fish, the bait, the equipment. Don't travel too far, don't go out for too long, let the children have the fun, make their fun your enjoyment. It is not about your catch—it is about theirs. If nothing is biting, move on. Add swimming, splashing, picnicking to the experience. Give them praise, not criticism. Help them to see the beauty of the lake, the river, the setting, the sounds, and the feeling of being there.

AGE OF GRANDCHILD: 3 and up

BEST SEASON: Spring is really good for hungry and aggressive panfish.

ALSO CHECK OUT:

Family Friendly Fishing Waters:
www.michigan.gov/dnr/0,4570,7-153-10364-299046--,00.html

General Michigan Fishing Information:
www.michigan.gov/dnr/0,1607,7-153-10364---,00.html

Michigan Fish and How to Catch Them:
www.michigan.gov/dnr/0,1607,7-153-10364-213908--,00.html

Michigan Fish Hatcheries: www.michigan.gov/dnr/0,4570,7-153-10364_52259_28277-271526--,00.html

Nobody can do for little children what grandparents do. ALEX HALEY

59

Grandparents Day

You may not know it, but Grandparents Day is a holiday, too. Ranking far below Mother's Day and Father's Day, this national holiday was established in 1973 through the efforts of Marian McQuade, a mother of 15 from West Virginia who was as dedicated to the care of senior citizens as she was to children. In her efforts to reach out to a generation of grandparents, she formed the Forget-me-not Ambassadors to ensure that senior homes were visited regularly. In 1978, President Jimmy Carter recognized this effort and ushered in a national day of commemoration.

President Carter's statements at the signing of the new legislation included the following: "Whether they are our own or surrogate grandparents who fill some of the gaps in our mobile society, our senior generation also provides our society a link to our national heritage and traditions."

The day did not get instant recognition, but there is hope that those of us in the baby boomer generation will demand that this day be as venerated as much as the other days that honor parenting in all its forms.

Grandparents Day occurs on the first Sunday after Labor Day, a day sure to be overlooked since it comes right after the last big holiday of summer, toward the beginning of school, and during the transition to the school year, autumn and family schedules. But don't allow it to be forgotten. Instead, make it a day that helps your grandchildren honor the life of a grandparent. Your children can help make this happen, but it can be a success if you do the planning, too.

This day is not for going somewhere, nor for outside entertainment. Have a cake, have a celebration, but concentrate on the things that made your childhood special. The baby boomers are the last generation to have a childhood without computers, VCRs, DVDs, CDs, color television. We grew up with empty lots, cardboard boxes, board games, books, and paper puzzles; show your grandchildren this and how much fun it can be.

Play some old board games—they are still around, just not as prevalent. Make a rocket ship out of a cardboard box. Gather everyone around and tell a story about your childhood and make this a day of photo album reminiscence—but not too much—let them leave wanting to see more, not hoping that you don't find another album.

If you have saved any old clothing, a little dress-up can go a long way, too. It might be good to pop some popcorn and gather around the old radio, too—if you were from the generation of radio dramas, you can now order them on tape or CD. Turn off all but one lamp and pull the easy chairs around the CD player. Have popcorn and lemonade and tune in to the old radio experience. Because we have put so much stimuli into our world, it takes a little effort to reduce the distractions and concentrate on the audio experience.

A WORD TO THE WISE:

Grandparents lived in a world where there were a variety of sensory experiences and we got more exercise than our thumbs on the Game Boy. The smell of popcorn and sound of radio are all part of that experience. But nothing is more nostalgic than the candy we ate as children. We have had a wonderful time getting boxes of old-time candy to share. Kids say, "What is that?" and our contemporaries say, "I remember eating that . . . "

AGE OF GRANDCHILD: All

BEST SEASON: First Sunday after Labor Day—make it an afternoon of fun!

CONTACT: Your place or your children's home—this needs a home atmosphere.

WEBSITE:

For old-time candy: www.oldtimecandy.com

See if they might have the assortment that brings back memories to your taste buds. Share this bit of your childhood with your grandchildren. We were flooded with nostalgia when we opened our first box, and we gave away numerous boxes to friends for Valentine's Day for the fun of sharing memories.

Grandparents and Grandchildren, together they create a
chain of Love linking the past with the future. UNKNOWN

60

Kirtland's Warblers

One rare treasure was found only in Michigan until very recently. It is tiny and requires the patience and dedication of the true treasure hunter. This treasure is not buried under the Sleeping Bear sand dunes, nor is it stored in a steel vault. This treasure lives and breathes and flies among the jack pine trees in central Michigan, in the Huron National Forest. This treasure is a bluish

gray-backed and yellow-bellied bird known as the Kirtland's warbler, and it is one of the rarest songbirds in North America. As of 2007, a survey of singing males (only the males sing) numbered 1,697. In 1987 that number was only 167.

The Kirtland's warbler's rarity is due to the very specific habitat it needs to nest and raise its young: dense stands of young jack pine forest, with trees between four and twenty years old. This type of forest is dependent on fire for rejuvenation, but once fires were suppressed because of human settlement, the trees began to age beyond their usefulness for the birds. The U.S. Forest Service put together a specific management plan that uses logging, planting, seeding, and controlled burns to create the most favorable and sustainable habitat for this special bird. And they have succeeded.

When you drive down Highway F-32 from Mio, Michigan, you will see signs on either side indicating that this is Kirtland's warbler habitat. The birds arrive from their winter range in the Bahamas around mid-May and get right down to the business of courtship and raising a family. They leave sometime in August, so this is a treasure hunt with a very specific time frame. Treasure hunters (bird watchers) aren't allowed to venture into the forest and must search from the side of the road, but it is possible to go on guided hikes led by Forest Service personnel into areas where the birds are known to live. Seeing one of these birds will be an unforgettable memory for you and your grandchildren, and one that they may be able to share in the same way with their grandchildren 50 years from now.

Bonding & Bridging

Bird watching is good for people of all ages, but the younger, the better, so start early with your grandchildren, when they are babies and toddlers, by watching the birds outside your windows. As they get older, let them help you fill your bird feeders and watch the birds come in. When you go for walks together, point out the kinds of birds you see—you don't have to know the names of all of them— just focus on five or six common ones to recognize. By the time they are seven or eight, you should be able to introduce them to binoculars (maybe a play pair to begin with). Using binoculars takes practice and can be frustrating for the beginner, but once they become comfortable, the world of birding is open to them and this observation means a greater awareness of everything.

A WORD TO THE WISE:

Take the self-guided, 58-mile auto tour and see the birds' summer home. There are 12 stops on the tour; look for otters, eagles, and trout, too. If you want to better your chances, go on a Forest Service guided tour between May 15 and July 2. Reservations aren't required and tours leave from Mio or Grayling at 7:30 a.m. with a charge of $10 per person. You follow a Forest Service employee in a car caravan and can leave the tour whenever you wish. The full tour lasts three hours, but your chances of seeing a singing Kirtland's warbler are good.

AGE OF GRANDCHILD: 8 to teenager

BEST SEASON: Spring and summer

CONTACT: Guided Kirtland's Warbler Tours: Mio Ranger District, 107 McKinley Rd., Mio, MI 48647-9314; (989) 826-3252; www.fs.usda.gov/detail/hmnf/passes-permits/?cid=STELPRDB5247524

U.S. Fish & Wildlife Service, East Lansing Field Office, 2651 Coolidge Rd., East Lansing, MI 48823; (517) 351-2555; www.fws.gov/midwest/EastLansing

ALSO CHECK OUT:

Kirtland's Warbler Festival: www.huronpines.org/festival

Michigan Audubon Kirtland's Warbler Tours: www.michiganaudubon.org/kirtlands-warbler-tours/

Point Pelee National Park, Canada: www.pc.gc.ca/pn-np/on/pelee/index_E.asp

Whitefish Point Bird Observatory: www.wpbo.org

Adopt the pace of nature: her secret is patience. RALPH WALDO EMERSON

61

Kite Flying

If you are looking for a simple activity that connects wind, energy, and flight, it is hard to beat a kite. If you are looking for something that is almost magic—build your own with string, ribbon, newspaper, and wood. Can you imagine those ingredients taking you into the atmosphere? How do you shape the kite? Why a tail? Do you run with the wind, against, or across? These questions have been pondered since 1000 BCE in China, and we still work with the same basic elements to make a sailboat move, support a parasail, or fly a hang glider.

I still have memories of a clear, sunny day with gusty winds on a hill when I was a child. There was a wonderful field of grass, surrounded by a boulevard of oak trees. My parents and grandparents had purchased a box kite, one of the first purchased kites I'd ever had. We assembled it and the excitement grew. The breeze blew. I ran and ran and ran, and it seemed as if I was destined to have the only earthbound kite in the park, but then it took flight and we were playing out the string, watching it rise, feeling the pull of the wind. We were tethered to flight and it was exhilarating, until finally it was time

to reel it in. The kite fought the command to return to the ground and as a last vestige of independence it found an oak tree. My grandfather and my father both thought that they could get it down. Now I wonder—is my dad's shoe still lodged in that oak branch?

We can put the material together, create the right design, and decorate the best-looking kite in the world, but to succeed we need wind. There is no better place for kite flying than on the shore of the Great Lakes where the cold air of the lake mixes with the warmer air over land and gives us some of the most dependable breezes in the world. The result is great kite flying and some spectacular new developments like kiteboarding or snowkiting on Lake St. Clair or the Great Lakes!

Bonding & Bridging

What is more pleasurable and simple than running across a grassy field, string in hand, and watching a kite take flight? This is the essence of the shared experience. It is not the amount of money we spend or any glitz or glamour that connects us with our grandchildren; instead, it is the quiet sharing of discovery. What is flight? What is wind? How did we learn to control the wind and rise to the sky? Does the kite teach us anything about flight? How perfect an opportunity to talk about Wilbur and Orville Wright, Leonardo da Vinci, and all the dreamers who led us to our modern planes and rockets. The kite is our thread to the sky. It was Ben Franklin's means to learn about lightning; maybe it is your means to explore your dreams about the universe. Check out the Great Lakes Kite Festival in Grand Haven on the shore of Lake Michigan for stunt kites, monster kites, and lots of special events and excitement. Kids can get caught up in the enthusiasm of these events and you can use that excitement to guide them to learn and experience more.

A WORD TO THE WISE:

We used to think of kites as a summer pastime, but extreme skiers and snowboarders now harness themselves to modified kites and are pulled, often airborne, across frozen lakes. Called snowkiting or kiteboarding, this combination of a clear frozen lake, preferably one covered with a base of snow—lets a skier catch the energy of the wind and literally fly across the surface. This is a great winter spectacle and can be observed in many places like Little Black Lake near Muskegon and Reed's Lake near Grand Rapids.

AGE OF GRANDCHILD: 3 and up

BEST SEASON: Spring and fall

ALSO CHECK OUT:

Great Lakes Kite Festival: www.mackite.com/glskc.htm

Great Lakes Kiteboarding: www.greatlakeskiteboarding.com/

Local Kite Spots: http://localkitespots.com/kitesurfing/Michigan

Lyon Township Kite Festival:
http://lyontwp.org/detail.php?ContentSection=Community&ContentID=326

At age seven, children have as passionate a longing for creative interactions and learning as they earlier had for explorations of the world. Joseph Chilton Pearce, The Magical Child

62

Libraries

Did you know that libraries are not an American invention or a creation of Mr. Carnegie? The Sumerians had a "House of Tablets." Imagine what it would have been like when everything was written on a clay tablet. The ancient Egyptians were one of the first cultures to create a "House of Books," and they are often credited with setting the standard for books for the rest

of civilization, even though books changed over time. This quest for knowledge was best exemplified by the Library of Alexandria, which was established in the third century BCE in Alexandria, Egypt. At its peak, the library was a regional center of learning and scholarship and housed many scrolls until its destruction.

While the U.S. doesn't have anything to compare with the Library of Alexandria, books have had strong supporters throughout our history. One such supporter—Andrew Carnegie—built 2,509 libraries between 1881 and 1917. His philanthropy mostly occurred in America, the British Isles and Canada. Public libraries like these have been one of the greatest successes for freedom of speech in the world. In Michigan there were 60 Carnegie grants and out of those, 28 are still in use as libraries, 11 were demolished, and 21 exist, but not as libraries. Can you find them?

Since that time, libraries have grown in many ways and some feature new, modern buildings, university and college libraries, and new e-libraries. All libraries are wonderful and offer great opportunities and treasures, but some also combine the excitement of a historic structure that means that the library is a story in itself. One of the most beautiful and exotic-looking libraries was built with lumber money in Saginaw—the Hoyt Main Library. Be sure to explore the building and its programs as well as the books.

Contrasting with the old classic libraries, like Detroit's Main Library, is the modern Gerald R. Ford library, which features the history of the U.S. during President Ford's 1974–1977 term in office. This is a modern building in Ann Arbor and provides a personal view of one of the leaders of our nation.

Bonding & Bridging

Even in the information age, books are still repositories of knowledge, feelings, and personal connections. You can see that in your young grandchildren who are excited by the story time the library offers and the excitement that comes with opening a new book or the comfort of opening one they know and love. A fundamental goal of libraries is to instill in people (especially children) a lifelong love of reading and provide learning opportunities through books and other media formats. Visiting a library together can foster a special relationship between the generations by bonding over the magic of a shared book. Grandparents have the patience to allow the child time to browse, to look, and to touch many volumes before making a choice, and then bring a book home to share. Perhaps the highlight of a grandchild's visit is that calm period of reading just before bed. It is a time when the book is a magical bridge between generations and across imaginations.

A WORD TO THE WISE:
Most libraries offer story time, when the librarians read selected books. The readers use great voices and sounds, incorporate music and often movement to interact with the children, and the book becomes a magical device to connect everyone. It is important to let your grandchildren know you are there with them. By participating, you show them you value reading, too.

AGE OF GRANDCHILD: All

BEST SEASON: Any season, but winter really seems the best time to bury oneself in the warmth and the cozy atmosphere of a library.

CONTACT: Detroit Public Library, Main Branch, 5201 Woodward Ave., Detroit, MI 48202; (313) 481-1300; www.detroit.lib.mi.us/branch/main

Gerald R. Ford Presidential Library, 1000 Beal Ave., Ann Arbor, MI 48109; (734) 205-0555; www.fordlibrarymuseum.gov

Gerald R. Ford Presidential Museum, 303 Pearl St. NW, Grand Rapids, MI 49504-5353; (616) 254-0400; www.fordlibrarymuseum.gov

Hoyt Main Library, Saginaw, 505 Janes Ave., Saginaw, MI 48607; (989) 755-0904; www.saginawlibrary.org

ALSO CHECK OUT:
Carnegie Libraries in Michigan:
https://en.wikipedia.org/wiki/List_of_Carnegie_libraries_in_Michigan

Children have never been very good at listening to their elders, but they have never failed to imitate them. JAMES BALDWIN

63

Lighthouses

How many lighthouses are there in Michigan? One list says there are 130, by far the most for any state! But then again, only one state has shorelines on four of the Great Lakes—a total of over 3,000 miles, including the island shores. No other state has over 1,000 miles. So, where do you start when you set out to explore the lighthouses? Which ones make for the best visits and have the most colorful lights?

The lighthouses that fit our romantic image and the images in the children's books are usually on a rugged coast or an island. They seem lonely but, of course, they were beacons of hope on storm-tossed coasts. Here, the heroic lighthouse keepers worked to keep their oil lamps lit and rescued survivors of ships that could not handle the tempests. Just their setting alone will inspire your grandchildren.

Many lighthouses on Michigan's shores can be reached by foot, and the walk is part of the pleasure because it creates the setting for the lighthouse. The lighthouse museums that are featured in this book are good places to start, but there are many other options.

We recommend that you go to whichever lighthouses are near your travels, but be sure to visit the following if you are looking for something special: Grand Traverse Lighthouse in Leelanau State Park includes a museum, and a well-preserved keeper's house. Point Betsie Lighthouse is the second-most-photographed lighthouse in the nation and is just south of Sleeping Bear Dunes National Lakeshore. South Manitou Island Lighthouse is only accessible by boat. Its 117 steps lead up to a classic view of Lake Michigan and is now it is part of the Sleeping Bear Dunes National Lakeshore. Stannard Rock is built on a rock island that is below the surface of the lake. Rock of Ages is on a barren, rocky island. Both are near Isle Royale and are classic open-water light towers. Holland Harbor South Pierhead or "Big Red" is a classic red brick building on a pier and is very picturesque. Eagle Harbor Lighthouse on the Keweenaw is another classic red building, but this one is on land.

Bonding & Bridging ⋈⋈⋈⋈⋈⋈⋈⋈⋈⋈⋈⋈⋈⋈⋈⋈

This way of life is no longer a choice for people seeking employment, but the need for lights is still great. Today we use radio signals, computers, and satellites to help our boats stay off the shores and rocks. These tools guide boats in fog and at night, in storms, and when they are in danger. The Great Lakes are large, beautiful and inviting, but they are also dangerous. There have been numerous shipwrecks in Great Lakes history, with 18 percent on Lake Superior, 23 percent on Lake Michigan, 23 percent on Lake Huron, 9 percent on Lake Ontario, and 27 percent on Lake Erie.

Today, we travel in many ways, and it might be good to share with the grandchildren how we have worked to make all these modes safer. Who are today's lighthouse keepers? Perhaps they are the air traffic controllers, the police directing traffic, or the forecaster at the weather service. We have road service, 911, and lots of things we can call on, but everything depends upon the individual making the best decisions in order to avoid dangerous situations.

As a grandparent, you share adventures with your grandchildren, but you are also their lighthouse keepers, watching for danger and willing to step in when needed. Their life is a voyage, and you are there to help them past some of the shoals of growing up.

A WORD TO THE WISE:

Each lake has significant lighthouses in parks, cities, and private locations. They are a colorful part of our history, but in many ways they are hard for children to understand. How can a big tower on land help ships at sea? Maybe you can help them see how our traffic lights work. From a distance we can see that it is clear to go or that we must stop. Because we can see light over open distances, we can use it for signals and safety.

AGE OF GRANDCHILD: 3 and up

BEST SEASON: Summer

ALSO CHECK OUT:

Eagle Harbor Lighthouse: www.keweenawhistory.org/sites/lighthouse.html

Grand Traverse Lighthouse: www.grandtraverselighthouse.com

Inventory of Michigan Lighthouses: www.michiganlighthouseguide.com

Point Betsie Lighthouse: www.pointbetsie.org

I don't intentionally spoil my grandkids. It's just that correcting them often takes more energy than I have left. Gene Perret

64

Michigan Weather

We often take issue with the weather and sometimes combat it on a daily basis. While we certainly need buildings to keep us dry and structures to protect us from hurricanes and storms, "bad" weather is really a gift of variety and opportunity.

Grandparents can help grandchildren avoid weather phobia and the tendency to stay glued to the Weather Channel, and avoid the constant critiquing of weather as too warm, too cold, too wet, too windy by helping them have fun in "bad" weather. Does it help to complain about the weather? Shouldn't we get the most out of all our experiences? Of course, we're not talking about ignoring tornadoes or other dangerous storms, nor are we referring to air quality indices caused by pollution. But think back to your childhood: Did you always want to come in when it rained? Did you want to be inside when

it was cold or snowy? We know our grandchildren would like to be out playing, no matter the weather, so here is the challenge to every grandparent: figure out the appropriate toys and special activities for the most challenging of weather.

Getting dirty is normal and not something to avoid. Do you remember running out in the rain, jumping in puddles, making mud pies? Many of these things don't happen now. Not because the kids wouldn't enjoy them, but because it is easier to bring the children inside. Small children think an umbrella is fun, and they like to walk with you in the rain. A big tree canopy is another form of umbrella, and it is amazing to see how much rain the leaves catch. Watch how the rain moves from leaf to leaf. Snowmen, snow forts, and snowballs can be fun, too. Study the snowflakes by putting a piece of black felt on a board. Let it get cold, then catch some and look at them with a magnifying glass.

For most of the year, "bad" weather is caused by two things—the wrong clothes and the wrong attitude. You can help change that. Give your grandchildren the gift of "bad" weather and you'll add many good days to their lives.

Bonding & Bridging

Everyone talks about the weather and, unfortunately, almost everyone complains about it. But what is weather? Of all the events in our world, this is one thing that your grandchildren can observe and study wherever they are. The purchase of a simple digital weather station means they can record temperature, heat, humidity, and rainfall.

Tell your grandchildren about the big storms you have seen. Tell them about John Muir, the great naturalist, who would tie himself to treetops in order to feel the wind. Talk about the coldest day you've experienced, and by comparison how it would probably be a warm day to a polar explorer or the Inuit. How hot is it for people on the equator and in the rainforest? What is the wettest, coldest, or windiest place in the world? These are exotic frontiers of weather and if we explore and explain them, each day is a new experience for our grandchildren and an opportunity for understanding and enjoyment.

A WORD TO THE WISE:

We do not want to belittle weather. It is important to dress correctly, and we need to know about sunscreen, windbreakers, rain jackets, and warm winter clothing. Children accept these if they understand why they are needed. Weather has only three ingredients—wind, temperature, and moisture—but think of how much variety can be created from those three elements!

AGE OF GRANDCHILD: 3 and up

BEST SEASON: All

ALSO CHECK OUT:

Great Lakes Weather and Climate:
www.great-lakes.net/envt/refs/weather.html

Michigan Climate Records:
www.usclimatedata.com/climate/michigan/united-states/3192

Michigan State Climatologist's Office: http://climate.geo.msu.edu/

National Oceanographic and Atmospheric Administration: http://noaa.gov/

Weather Michigan: www.weathermichigan.com

*Grandparents somehow sprinkle a sense
of stardust over grandchildren.* ALEX HALEY

65

Petoskey Stones

We all love to pick rocks and skip stones, but like most prospectors, we want to find something special. Here is the ultimate treasure hunt—searching for the elusive Petoskey stone, Michigan's state stone!

This is not a joke—there is a Petoskey stone. It is a unique fossilized coral. Primarily made of the mineral calcite, it is easy to polish and carve, with wonderful lines that were created by the growth of coral polyps in an ancient ocean. This six-sided fossil colony coral (*Hexagonaria percarinata*) is perhaps

more enjoyed for its unusual features than its beauty, but that does not make it any less desirable.

Originally this coral formed in the warm seas of the Devonian Period, more than 350 million years ago. Today we can thank the continental glaciers for picking up pieces of these fossils, polishing them, rounding them and depositing them where we can find them as small stones that fit in our pockets.

The name of the stone is supposed to be based on the name of an Ottawa (Odawa) chief. The city of Petoskey gets its name from the same place, and the name is a phonetic attempt at recreating the much more complicated Ottawa language. The translation means "rays of the rising sun."

The stone was part of an elaborate coral complex and is therefore a fossil of a living organism. It is only one of many fossils that have eroded from the area's limestone after being moved by glaciers and shaped by the waves. Keen eyes can discern the honeycomb pattern. Of course, this is not the only treasure of the Michigan shores. Here you can find Lake Superior agates, beautiful greenstones, fossils like horned, chained and honeycomb corals, and even exotic Frankfurt Green and Leland Blue, which are remnants of smelting and examples of the area's early history.

While the Petoskey stone can be found on Lake Huron shores, too, the best hunting is from Ludington to Petoskey (but no collecting is allowed at Sleeping Bear Dunes National Lakeshore).

Bonding & Bridging ⨯⨯⨯⨯⨯⨯⨯⨯⨯⨯⨯⨯⨯⨯⨯⨯⨯⨯⨯⨯⨯

Something older than we are! You can't ask for something better! Take your time and find a nice place to enjoy rocks of all sorts. Make piles, sort them by texture, color, and shape. Then skip the rocks if you are by the water. What better reason could there be for collecting rocks? Find the flat ones, find ones that fit your hand, and then throw them and watch as they bound across the surface of the water. Have contests, have fun!

Remember a few things that will make your day more fun—first, collect on the way back. Walk to the farthest point before searching. Why carry rocks out and back? Second, bring water to spray on the rocks to see their true potential and bring fine sandpaper to bring out the beauty. And if your grandchildren really get into rocks, there is the Petosky Stone Festival in Barnes County Park near Eastport.

A WORD TO THE WISE:

You can buy Petoskey stones, but buying them is not as much fun as finding your own. However, if you buy a few as samples, it will be easier for your grandchildren to envision what you are looking for. One way to get your grandchildren interested is to structure their first Petoskey stone hunt like an Easter egg hunt. Hide a few around your home for them to find. This will teach them how to search, observe, and discriminate. Add a few other stones around the yard, too. It will become a game and they might even ask you to take them out and hide them again. This will help them get ready to find Petoskey stones on the beach.

AGE OF GRANDCHILD: 7 and up

BEST SEASON: Spring, after the ice has pushed more stones onto the beach.

ALSO CHECK OUT:

Rock Collecting in the Upper Peninsula:
www.exploringthenorth.com/rocks/collect.html

Rockhound Destinations:
www.copperagates.com/home/rockhound_destinations

Michigan Rockhounding Locations:
www.michrocks.org/rockin-fun/michigan-locations/mich-loc.html

Michigan Rocks and Minerals:
www.mwminerals.com/Michigan_Minerals_Gallery.html

Grandparents are similar to a piece of string—handy to have around and easily wrapped around the fingers of their grandchildren. UNKNOWN

66

Picking Cherries

In Japan, the cherry symbolizes happiness. So much so, that on their wedding day, a bride and groom drink a beverage made from cherry blossoms. It just seems that this is a fruit that makes people smile. And what other fruit is so connected to the mythology of our country? George Washington didn't get into trouble cutting down an apple tree—no, it was a cherry tree.

Cherries have brought happiness to Michigan farmers and consumers for over 150 years. Now, 75 percent of the country's tart cherries and 20 percent of the sweet cherries are grown in this state. That works out to be around 200 million to 250 million pounds of cherries. Traverse City, which calls itself "Cherry Capital of the World," got its start when a Protestant missionary living on Old Mission Peninsula began to harvest and sell the ruby fruit. The trees had actually been planted much earlier in what is now known as Detroit by French settlers who brought them to this country for their gardens.

Today, there are 65 cherry orchards in the northwest region near Lake Michigan, since the climate along the lake (warm days/cool nights) is especially conducive to the production of this fruit. Along many roadsides there are stands with boxes of beautiful cherries for sale. Some sellers create artistic patterns with dark burgundy cherries next to the red and gold Queen Anne's cherries. It's easy to go crazy over cherries when you see them so beautifully arranged.

While it's possible to take a Sunday drive and stop at one of the farm stands stationed along the backroads, we suggest a hands-on approach. There will be cherries that all ages can pick, and your labor (which doesn't really feel like work) has the wonderful reward of a sweet and tart taste in your mouth at the end of the day. Let the children know that a full tree's production of cherries could make about 28 pies. The average American eats about one pound of cherries per year and the tart cherries (eaten dried, frozen, or in juice) have extremely high levels of antioxidants and beta-carotene, so they really are nature's health food. Your grandchildren will be excited seeing their buckets fill up and you will be introducing them to a wonderfully healthy fruit.

Traverse City hosts a National Cherry Festival the second week of July. Check out the Teddy Bear Tea, bicycle rodeo, pet contest, bubble-gum blowing contest, and, naturally, a contest or two to see who can eat the most cherry pie.

Bonding & Bridging

There are native cherries you can collect with your grandchildren to make jams and jellies. Chokecherry, pin cherry, and sand cherry shrubs all produce a wonderful fruit, but do not let them sample these until they've been cooked, since they are not naturally sweet like the domestic variety. Collecting the cherries and then working together in the kitchen to make a sweet concoction that goes onto bread or toast or over ice cream is a guaranteed memory maker. If you have been to the cherry orchards and picked some baskets together, you can make a pie. Or show them how easy it is to wash the cherries and lay them flat on a tray or cookie sheet, stick them in the freezer, and bag them up the next day. Then when February comes around and everyone is dreaming of those lovely summer months, take a couple frozen cherries out, let them thaw a bit, pop them in your mouth and smile with the memory and taste of summer.

A WORD TO THE WISE:

You can eat the cherries as you pick them, but it is best to wash them first. Cherries are one of the most heavily sprayed fruits. Even though we were told by the grower that it was safe to eat them right off the tree, all the cherries had a white, chalky coating on them. Ask where you can wash them after you pick them. Most places will have a hose. You'll notice that many fruit stands have signs that state, "Washed Cherries." It's very hard not to eat the cherries while you pick them, but tell the kids they aren't safe to eat until they've been washed.

AGE OF GRANDCHILD: 3 to teenager

BEST SEASON: Summer

CONTACT: National Cherry Festival: www.cherryfestival.org

North Star Organics: http://northstarorganics.com

Michigan Cherries: www.michiganagriculture.com/foods/michigan-cherries/

Michigan Pick-Your-Own-Cherry Farms: www.pickyourown.org/MI.htm

If nothing is going well, call your grandmother. ITALIAN PROVERB

67

Picnicking

Let's have a picnic—it's a simple phrase, but it had so much meaning when I was growing up. It meant we were going to a park where I could explore, and it probably meant that we would be meeting my grandparents.

A picnic always meant packing food and dishes in a basket, bringing the charcoal and a tablecloth. Why is a picnic tablecloth always a red checkerboard pattern? Of course, there would be a cooler for cold dishes and some pop. Then my grandmother would come with a hotdish wrapped in a dish towel. She had it wrapped almost like a turban—I still don't know how she did it, but that towel somehow managed to keep the dish and its contents hot for 50 miles!

This was a wonderful setting. We would greet each other, bring out the food and sit and eat in fresh air, surrounded by green plants and open space. It was a paradise of opportunity for an inner-city child. After the food was leisurely consumed, it would be time to sit in a folding chair, or go for a short walk. Grandpa would usually accompany me on this stroll—"letting the food settle" was the code phrase for it.

Picnicking is one of the real simple pleasures that gets overlooked in our fast-food, fast-service, fast-paced lives, but perhaps it is the antidote we need most. Spill something? So what? Get food on your clothing—no big deal. Leave the hang-ups from home at home. Relax. Eat with your fingers! Crack open the watermelon and spit the seeds.

Don't bring fast foods to a picnic. A real picnic involves preparation and anticipation. It's a meal, time to roam, time to talk, maybe take a swim, and then to revisit the leftovers.

If you do not have the time to prepare a picnic, it is a good excuse to visit a deli or specialty food diner. Instead of going home and eating in front of the television, pick up your favorite food from a deli and then head to the park. Take your time and enjoy the setting, the people, and the flavors of food eaten in the fresh air.

Bonding & Bridging

The old adage that the way to a man's heart is through his stomach goes for just about everyone, especially our grandchildren. A picnic is all about the setting and comfort foods. What is it that we like about certain foods? Beans in a brown crock will always be perfect, but a picnic needs watermelon to make it great. Let the grandchildren help with planning and preparation. See what makes it perfect for them and why. Do you cook brats, roast marshmallows, eat cold foods, or put a fire to the shish kabobs?

Cooking with fire provides you with a way to teach safety with fire and heat. There are many options from grills to open fires, and each helps children learn about cooking and basic survival skills. An appreciation of tradition, food, setting, and preparation may follow and these picnics might become a treasured memory, as they are for our generation.

A WORD TO THE WISE:

Even the word "picnic" is unusual—it first was known as a "pique-nique" in France and later, in the 1800s, as a "picnic" in England. Originally it was a gathering like a family reunion (potluck). Later, after the French Revolution, "pique-niques" switched to open-air parks as a celebration of freedom. In England, the Picnic Society formed for a short period. The group would gather with food from all the participants and no particular host. The German version is "picknick." In 1989, the PanEuropean Picnic took place and was a famous gathering and protest to reunify Germany. All these versions share one similarity: they are ways to gather large groups without having to open your house or cook all the food. What an excellent idea!

AGE OF GRANDCHILD: All

BEST SEASON: Spring, summer, or fall, but don't rule out a winter picnic, which can really be fun if you prepare and dress for it.

ALSO CHECK OUT:

Picnic Recipe Ideas:
www.countryliving.com/food-drinks/g783/picnic-recipes-0609

Michigan State Parks: www.michigandnr.com/parksandtrails/#list

Pictured Rocks National Lakeshore: www.nps.gov/piro/index.htm

Sleeping Bear Dunes National Lakeshore: www.nps.gov/slbe/index.htm

Now that I've reached the age where I need my children more than they need me, I really understand how grand it is to be a grandmother. Mrs. Margaret Whitlam

68

Pow Wows

No one knows how pow wows began, although there are many theories. The word "pow wow" is believed to be from the Narragansett tribe and refers to a curing ceremony. Some think that pow wows were started by the war dances of the Ponca. A website about First Nations people in Canada reads, "Songs and dances that signified spirituality and religion were used in ceremonies.

Upon seeing these ceremonies, the early European explorers thought 'pow wow' was the whole dance when it actually referred to healers and spiritual leaders by the Algonian phrase *Pau Wau.*"

I am filled with pleasure at a pow wow; here I see happiness displayed in dance and music, conversation and action. Native regalia are an expression of continuity and promise. There is no replacing the experience. For your grandchildren and you, attending a pow wow is like being transported to another world.

Pow wows consist of social dances that have special meanings for the nations and their histories. From the very beginning, your grandchildren will be captivated. As the Grand Entry begins the pow wow, the eagle staff leads a flag procession (of the tribal nation, the United States flag, the Prisoner of War flag, and the military flags) carried with great reverence. The flags are followed by the dancers—first the men, then the women.

The intensity of a pow wow is unmatched. Your grandchildren will feel the drumbeat and may even get a sense of traveling back in time, as the music combines history, religion, and social norms. The singers are important members of the American Indian society; the drums are sacred and passed on to each generation. Old songs are mixed with new songs, elders sit beside youth at the drums, and the dance includes participants of all ages and genders. Some feel that the drum is the heartbeat, an answer to the vibrations of the Creator's first thoughts as the world was created.

Every part of the pow wow is done in a sacred circle that is inclusive and represents the circle of life. Veterans, elders, princesses, and organizers are all honored, and everyone is made to feel welcome. The rules are simple—no profanity, no drugs and alcohol, no cutting across the dance circle, and ask before taking photos. A pow wow is one experience that your grandchild and you will never forget.

Bonding & Bridging

The United States is known as the "melting pot" for good reason. Our country consists of diverse groups, varying cultures and many different backgrounds. A pow wow is an excellent chance to expose your grandchildren to the traditions of the indigenous peoples of America. In Canada they are referred to as the First Nations. Here, you can watch these proud people celebrate their cultural identity.

Ask your grandchildren what they think about their identity. (This is a tough concept, so help them with a few examples but don't give them the answer you want to hear.) Ask what traditions they celebrate. What are the special days and events that mark their year and tell about their family and home? It is also a time to remind them that, like the people at the pow wow, we should celebrate all those who came before us and all life around us.

A WORD TO THE WISE:

Here are some pow wows to put on your calendar:

Late August: Rendezvous at the Straits Powwow: www.saintignace.org/event/rendezvous-at-the-straits-powwow/

End of August: Annual Kee-Boon-Mein-Kaa Pow Wow: www.pokagonpowwow.com/

Mid-October: Land of Falling Waters Traditional Pow Wow, Jackson

AGE OF GRANDCHILD: All

BEST SEASON: Summer and fall

ALSO CHECK OUT:

Crazy Crow Listing of Michigan Pow Wows: www.crazycrow.com/site/pow-wows-in-michigan/

Upcoming Michigan Pow Wows: www.cmich.edu/office_provost/OID/NAP/Pages/Upcoming-Michigan-Pow-wows.aspx

Pow Wow Etiquette: http://indiancountrytodaymedianetwork.com/2014/03/29/pow-wow-etiquette-10-rules-follow-and-out-arena-154195

My grandkids believe I'm the oldest thing in the world.
And after two or three hours with them, I believe it, too. Gene Perret

69

Urban Parks

As we explored the communities of Michigan and looked for the places we would want to share with our grandchildren, we often found our gaze settling on the urban parks, and found that the state has an amazing array of parks and opportunities. Then we considered how often people pack up and take to the road to discover the state parks, but seldom think about visiting parks in other communities. Maybe we are all missing one of the great assets of the state.

Urban parks tread a fine line between nature and society, between escape from the pressures of work and the people who make up the urban fabric. The parks we are looking for are not the traditional recreation parks—the ball diamonds and playgrounds—but those unique threads of nature that provide a sense of balance.

Originally urban parks were designed to give relief to the congestion of the Industrial Revolution. They needed trees, breeze, and water to serve as the

community's lungs. Park planners like Frederick Law Olmstead (Central Park, New York) found they could do much for the health of the community, the citizens, and our culture. The result can be found in places like Belle Isle in Detroit, where an island provides opportunities for fishing, hiking, picnicking, and playing, and which features a zoo, a conservatory, and bird watching opportunities. Campus Martius Park in downtown Detroit is one of the top urban parks in the country; it's the city's green space for meeting, relaxing, and renewal.

Saginaw is an example of how the smaller cities have created wonderful green spaces that provide a variety of experiences for all generations. Located along the Saginaw River are Ojibwa Island Park, Wickes Park and nearby Hoyt Park, all near the excellent Children's Zoo at Celebration Square, the Japanese Culture Center and Tea House, and the Andersen Enrichment Center.

Battle Creek Linear Park, situated along the Battle Creek River, provides opportunities for bicycling, fishing, in-line skating, and bird watching. There's also a series of interpretive signs to help you understand what you are enjoying. There are even loops built into this wonderful recreation system that incorporate 26 miles of paved trail, with the community and its amenities near each road junction.

Bonding & Bridging

Our grandchildren have a complicated world to navigate. The human environment requires us to understand economics and urban planning, while the natural environment reminds us that we rely on both fresh water and fresh air every day of our lives. So how do we coexist with the other parts of nature? Parks provide a good opportunity for this. Here, we can see how animals have adjusted, how plants continue to grow, how fish swim in the waters. Are these species aware of us? How many people in the buildings near the parks know the animals that call this place home?

Is it possible for us to live with nature? What makes a good city? How can we make choices that affect the survival of other animals and still live a good life? Is there anything more important than clean water and clean air? Each generation sees humanity's footprint increase and nature's reserves shrink. You have the chance to show your grandchildren what the world once was and then emphasize how important their decisions will be!

A WORD TO THE WISE:

Urban parks give you a unique opportunity to stop at playgrounds, take along picnic items, and choose paths with a variety of lengths, but perhaps the other unique feature is the ability to wander off into the community. Try deviating from the trail to buy lunch at a local diner. Hike off to check out a museum, get an ice cream cone, find a bakery, get candy. Integrate the two aspects of urban parks into an exciting combination. Reward your grandchildren when they see ten different birds or plants with a treat from a local vendor. This is not a trip based on endurance; it is an adventure in blending with nature and the city.

AGE OF GRANDCHILD: 3 and up

BEST SEASON: Spring, summer and fall

ALSO CHECK OUT:

Battle Creek Linear Park: www.bcparks.org/134/Linear-park

Belle Isle Park: www.belleisleconservancy.org

Campus Martius Park: www.campusmartiuspark.org

Muskegon County Parks: http://muskegoncountyparks.org

Saginaw Parks: www.saginaw-mi.com/pdfs/ParksList.pdf

It's funny what happens when you become a grandparent. You start to act all goofy and do things you never thought you'd do. It's terrific. MIKE KRZYZEWSKI

70

Waterfalls

If water and rocks are two of the basic elements of childhood creativity, a waterfall has to be the natural extension of our inspiration. The tumbling waters over a rock face, the white patterns, and the soothing sounds all make for a wonderful opportunity to take photos, draw, play in the water, and generally enjoy the wonder of nature. It is not surprising that the Ojibwa people (Chippewa) heard Manitou—the great mystery or spirit—in the tumbling waters. It was a voice of the land itself, the resonance of land and water.

Waterfalls are abundant in northern Michigan, especially the Upper Peninsula; one publication lists 219 different falls! Some are remote, some are small, and some just do not get visited. Does a two-foot falls count? Does a dam count?

There are some waterfalls that everyone visits—like Tahquamenon, and in a separate section we will recommend that, too. But in many ways it is the small and secluded waterfalls that can be the most fun. Here are two examples.

Memorial Falls, just outside of Munising, is an easy hike with a very small stream that does not seem to have any spectacular potential. But follow the short trail and it finds a 30-foot drop over an amphitheater of sandstone. From the top, the little stream just seems to disappear and you have to decide if you want to climb down and find it again.

Then there is Canyon Falls, which you reach by a trail from a roadside park on US-41. The parking lot gives no indication of the adventure ahead. The trail drops down through a wonderful sample of U.P. forests and then follows the Sturgeon River as it heads toward the canyon.

You can see the falls from above, or you can work your way down the stepped rock layers to see the 15-foot drop with water plunging over the upper layer of rock and then zig-zagging to the canyon bottom. If you are ambitious there are two more waterfalls beyond, but the challenge is not to see everything. It is to enjoy everything you see!

Bonding & Bridging

We can share many things with our grandchildren, including a sense of discovery; this is something that marks our movement through life, as well as the journey of history. The way to enhance a sense of discovery is to avoid the anticipation. Don't tell your grandchild what will be at the end of the trail, let them find out. In fact, let them show you.

If you know there is a waterfall, that is fine, but a "let's see what we can find" approach creates greater excitement and even encourages discovering more than the falls itself. The children will try to show you discoveries as you go, and then, when the waterfall comes, they will be so pleased to say, "Look, Grand . . . A waterfall!" This way, the children have ownership over the event and they feel a sense of discovery and pride. Those are good things, and you can build on them to create the self-esteem the child will need to make it through life.

Share their enthusiasm. Talk about how important water is and how we have to take care of it. Let them see the waterfall as a symbol for quality of life. Listen to the falls and hear a sound of the Earth.

A WORD TO THE WISE:

Another place to look for waterfalls is the Keweenaw Peninsula. There are some small falls right next to the road that are easy to observe. Jacob's Falls is very easy to see, but it's also an impressive drop, while Silver River Falls requires a very short walk from the bridge. Falls like these are simple to observe and you can float sticks and watch them go. As simple as that sounds, it is the beginning of learning about currents and flow. A little play can lead to a lot of knowledge.

AGE OF GRANDCHILD: All

BEST SEASON: Spring for the big flows, summer for gentler waters where you can find some places to play.

CONTACT: Michigan Waterfalls:
www.gowaterfalling.com/waterfalls/maps/statemichigan.shtml

ALSO CHECK OUT:

Sable Falls, Pictured Rocks National Lakeshore:
www.nps.gov/piro/index.htm

Upper and Lower Tahquamenon Falls:
www.michigandnr.com/parksandtrails/Details.aspx?type=SPRK&id=428

Teaching children about the natural world should be treated as one of the most important events in their lives. Thomas Berry, Dream of the Earth

71

Winter Festivals

Northerners have always taken pride in their ability to survive extreme weather. We flaunt windchill like a badge of honor. *What? Twenty below is not cold enough for you? Let me tell you about the windchill. Do you know what that means? It means that if you stood naked and let the wind blow over your body, you would freeze faster than if the wind did not blow. And why would we stand naked? Well, you've heard of a sauna, haven't you?*

To make sure our grandchildren take the same pride in winter, we have to take them outside and celebrate the season of snow, cold, and ice. We can engage in the frolics of winter—King Boreas is still alive in the frozen tundra! We ice fish (the true Northerner does not need an icehouse), snowshoe, hike, sled, cross-country ski, and snowmobile. We celebrate the clear blue sky, the snow-draped conifers, and the tracks in the forest. This is our element.

Others worry about earthquakes, hurricanes, tornadoes, and tsunamis; we worry that the next blizzard might miss us. That is the essence of the Winter Carnival, the Winter Festival. We carve palaces out of ice, make s'mores over a winter campfire, bowl with frozen turkeys, ride in horse-drawn sleighs, and crown ice royalty.

Our canine companions often join us, too, in dogsled races or demonstrations, or when skijoring. Like our furry friends, we are ready to run wild in the snow and across ice-covered lakes. In winter, waterfalls become sculptures, forest floors are chalkboards littered with animal tracks, and leafless trees sway in the winter wind like cheerleaders for those who appreciate the healthy, brisk winter environment. And though we may be bundled up and look like Weebles, we are filled with laughter and sport rosy cheeks. Winter is the essence of the North Country experience.

Bonding & Bridging

Grandparents grew up before the advent of electronics and before technology took over entertainment. We experienced a time of simpler games and entertainments. We found our fun in snowdrifts and piles of leaves, in floating branches downstream, and trying to catch snowflakes on our tongues. Ours was not a simpler time, but a time with a different definition of entertainment. Those pleasures transfer from age to age, if they are given a chance to flourish. Our task is to expose the new generation to past pleasures.

A WORD TO THE WISE:

Sled dogs hold a special place in our culture. Seeing a sled dog team working together elicits a feeling of winter joy and companionship and often translates the same emotions to the human observer. Many winter festivals include "mushers" and some have sled races, while others have rides. After such a festival, relive your adventures with hot chocolate and a movie like *Eight Below*, *Iron Will*, *Born to Run*, *Balto*, *Kevin of the North*, *Snow Dogs*, or *Chilly Dogs*.

AGE OF GRANDCHILD: All

BEST SEASON: Winter

ALSO CHECK OUT:

Michigan Ice Fest (ice climbing in Pictured Rocks): www.michiganicefest.com

Dog Sled Races

January, Camp Rotary Race: www.midunionsledhaulers.com

February, Fort Custer Recreation Area: www.midunionsledhaulers.com

February, Mystic Lake YMCA: www.midunionsledhaulers.com

February, Thunder Bay Classic: www.midunionsledhaulers.com

February, U.P. 200: http://up200.org/schedule/

Winter Festivals

Heikinpaiva, Mid-Winter Festival: www.finnishamericanreporter.com/heikinpaiva

Hunter Ice Festival: http://uncoverniles.com/festivals-events/hunter-ice-festival/

Life is no brief candle to me. It is a sort of splendid torch which I've got hold of for the moment and I want to make it burn as brightly as possible before handing it on to the future generations. GEORGE BERNARD SHAW

Index

A

A. E. Seaman Mineral Museum 91
Abbott Magic Company 28-29
Adventure Tour, Historic Mill Creek Discovery Park ....
  60-61
airplanes (Air Zoo)... 30-31
Allen's Root Beer Drive-In restaurant, Coldwater 116
American Indians (See also Ojibwa Indians)
  burial site, near Grand Rapids 110
  pow wows 148-149
Amphibiville, Detroit Zoo 18
Amtrak 96-97
Ann Arbor, places to visit in 104-105, 122-123, 136-137
arboretum 39, 104
art museums 98-99
Au Sable Lighthouse 78
Au Sable River, canoeing on 108
automobiles
  Ford Rouge Factory Tour.................................. 24-25
  Greenfield Village... 20-21
  Henry Ford Museum.. 22-23
A&W root beer stands...117

B

SS Badger (car ferry) 124
Baraga, Canyon Falls at...152
Barnes County Park, Petoskey stone festival in 143
Battle Creek
  Field of Flight Air Show and
    Balloon Festival in..................................... 126, 127
  urban park in 150
Bavarian festivals...44
Bay Mills, lighthouse at 73
beaches
  hunting for Petoskey stones on............... 100, 142-143
  Pictured Rocks National Lakeshore 78-79
  visits to 100-101
Belle Isle, Detroit 26-27
Belle Isle Park, Detroit...................................... 104, 150
berry picking 75, 144-145
"Big Red" Lighthouse 138
biking
  benefits of..102
  Mackinac Island 58, 59
  recommended trails for.............................. 102-103
  Seney National Wildlife Refuge........................ 74-75
bird watching
  Kirtland's Warblers 132-133
  Whitefish Point Bird Observatory 68-69, 73
boat rides/boats
  ferry across Lake Michigan 124-125
  Fort Wilkins Historic State Park...........................92
  Isle Royale National Park..................................94
  Locks at Sault Ste. Marie...................................66
  Pictured Rocks National Lakeshore 79
botanical gardens 104-105
Brockway Mountain Drive 93
butterfly gardens 18, 36-37

C

Calumet, Keweenaw National Historical Park in ... 90-91
Campfire Girls (Camp Fire USA) 106
campfires 106-107
camping...78-79, 86-87, 108
Campus Martius Park 150
Canadian Locks, at Sault Ste. Marie 66
canoeing 108-109
  Isle Royale National Park...................................94
  Sylvania Wilderness 86-87, 108
Canyon Falls, Baraga 152
carousels
  Greenfield Village..20
  Nelis' Dutch Village 34
Carp River 82, 83
catch-and-release fishing 128-129
cemeteries, visits to 110-111
Charles H. Wright Museum of African American
  History 14-15
Cheboygan, Swedish cemetery in.............................110
cherry picking 144-145
children's museums 112-113
Cliffs Shaft Mine 83
Clyde's Drive-In restaurant, Sault St. Marie 116
Coldwater, drive-in restaurant in 116
Colon, magic shops in 28-29
Colonial Michilimachinac.................................... 62-63
conservatories
  butterfly gardens............................... 18, 36-37
  Matthaei Conservatory and Nichols Arboretum.....104
cooking... 114-115
  campfire cooking..107
  with cherries 144-145
  with open fires, picnicking and 147
Copper mining, Keweenaw Peninsula................... 90-91
Copper World, Calumet 91
Curious Kids Museum, St. Joseph 112

D

Dearborn
  Ford Rouge Factory Tour.................................. 24-25
  Greenfield Village... 20-21
  Henry Ford Museum.. 22-23
Deklomp Wooden Shoe and Delft Factory, Holland ...34
Delaware Copper Mine, Calumet................................91
Detroit
  places to visit in........... 14-19, 26-27, 98-99, 104-105,
    112-113, 136-137
  urban parks in 150
Detroit Children's Museum 112
Detroit Institute of Art (DIA).............................. 98-99
Detroit Public Library, Main Branch 136-137
Detroit Zoo 18-19
  butterfly garden at..36
Discovery Center, Marquette 112
discovery park, Historic Mill Creek 60-61
dog sled races/teams.. 154, 155
Domino Farms, Petting Farm at 122-123
Dossin Great Lakes Museum 26-27
drive-in restaurants 116-117

E

Eagle Harbor Lighthouse 138
Eastport, Petoskey stone festival near 143
Edmund Fitzgerald (freighter)............................... 72-73
Empire, Sleeping Bear Dunes National Lakeshore . 54-55
ethnic celebrations 118-119
events, see festivals/events

F

Fab Magic Company 28, 29
factory tours 24-25
farm life 122-123
farmers markets 120-121
    farm life and 123
Father Marquette 58
Fayette Historic State Park 76-77
ferry rides.. 124-125
festivals/events
    African World festival..15
    Battle Creek Field of Flight Air Show and Balloon
    Festival 126, 127
    Bay City Fireworks Festival 126, 127
    ethnic celebrations.. 118-119
    Fayette's Heritage Day 76
    firework displays.. 126-127
    in Frankenmuth 44-45
    Great Lakes Kite Festival 135
    Interlochen Center for the Arts 50-51
    Mackinac Island 58, 59
    in Marquette 81, 85
    National Cherry Festival..144
    Noel Night 15
    Petoskey stone festival..143
    Subaru Noquemanon Ski Marathon.......................85
    Tulip Time Festival...34
    winter celebrations 154-155
fireworks 126-127
fish hatchery 56-57
fishing 86-87, 128-129
flower gardens.. 34-35
food
    campfire cooking...107
    cherries... 144-145
    cooking together.. 114-115
    drive-in restaurants...................................... 116-117
    from farmers markets 120-121
Ford Rouge Factory Tour 24-25
forests, see National Forests
Forget-me-not Ambassadors....................................130
Fort Wilkins Historic State Park 92-93
fossil coral (Petoskey Stones)...................... 100, 142-143
Frankenmuth, festivals in.................................... 44-45
Frederik Meijers Gardens and Sculpture Park
    butterfly garden at...36
    children's garden at 38-39

G

Garden, Fayette Historic State Park at 77
gardens
    botanical... 104-105
    butterfly 18, 36-37
    Lena Meijer Children's Garden........................... 38-39
    sculpture..36-37, 46-47
    tulip 34-35

Geology Trail, at Michigan Iron Industry Museum......83
Gerald R. Ford Library 136-137
Grand Haven
    firework displays in 126
    Great Lakes Kite Festival in 135
Grand Marais, lighthouses at 78
Grand Rapids, places to visit in 36-39, 98-99, 110
Grand Rapids Art Museum (GRAM) 98-99
Grand Traverse Lighthouse 138
Grandparents Day 130-131
Grayling area, activities in................ 108, 122, 123, 133
Great Lakes coastline 100-101
Great Lakes Shipwreck Museum........................... 72-73
Great Manistique Swamp...74
Greenfield Village 20-21
guided tours, in Huron National Forest....................133

H

Hall of Fame, U.S. Ski & Snowboard.................. 84-85
Hartwick Pines State Park and Logging Museum .. 48-49
health issues
    cherry picking, chemical sprays and 144-145
    sea sickness, preventing..125
    sunburn, preventing 101
Henry Ford Museum 22-23
Herschell-Spillman Carousel...................................20
Hexagonaria percarinata (fossil coral) 100, 142-143
hiking
    Hartwick Pines State Park 48-49
    Isle Royale National Park................................. 94-95
    Pictured Rocks National Lakeshore 78-79
    in Presque Isle area...88
    in Sylvania Wilderness................................. 86-87
Historic Mill Creek Discovery Park 60-61
Holland
    firework displays in 126
    places to visit in 34-35
Holland Harbor South Pierhead Lighthouse.............138
Holt cemetery, Morley..110
Houghton, Isle Royale National Park.................... 94-95
Hoyt Main Library, Saginaw 136-137
Hoyt Park, Saginaw...150
Huron National Forest..132

I

IMAX theater, Michigan Science Center 16, 17
Interlochen Center for the Arts............................. 50-51
Ishpeming
    Cliffs Shaft Mine...83
    U.S. Ski & Snowboard Hall of Fame 84-85
Isle Royale, lighhouses near......................................138
Isle Royale National Park...................................... 94-95

J

Jacob's Falls, Keweenaw Peninsula............................153

K

Kalamazoo Nature Center 32-33
Keweenaw National Historic Park 90-91
Keweenaw Peninsula
    copper mining on 90-91
    Fort Wilkins Historic State Park on.................... 92-93
    lighthouse on...138
    waterfalls on...153
Kid-Sense Garden 38-39

kindergarten, origins of..105
Kirtland's Warblers.. 132-133
kite flying 134-135
kiteboarding... 134, 135

L
Lake Express Carferry 124-125
Lake Michigan, ferry across 124-125
Lake of the Clouds..88
Lake Superior Shoreline Trail...................................88
lakeshores. See beaches; national lakeshores
Lansing
  drive-in restaurant in 116
  places to visit in 39-43
Lena Meijer Children's Garden 38-39
libraries... 136-137
lighthouses... 138-139
  at Grand Marais 78
  at Great Lakes Shipwreck Museum.................... 72-73
  at Marquette... 80-81
Linear Park, Battle Creek....................................150
living history
  Colonial Michilimackinac 62-63
  farm life...122
  Frankenmuth festivals................................. 44-45
  Greenfield Village..................................... 20-21
  Mackinac Island 58-59
Locks at Sault Ste. Marie, The 66-67
Log Slide, Pictured Rocks National Lakeshore.............78
logging... 48-49

M
Mackinac Island.. 58-59
Mackinac Island, fireworks display on 126
Mackinaw City, Historic Mill Creek Discovery Park ....
  60-61
magic stores 28-29
Manistee River, canoeing on 108
Manitou (tall ship) 52
Marquette
  children's museum in 112
  Subaru Noquemanon Ski Marathon.......................85
Marquette Maritime Museum........................... 80-81
Marshall M. Fredericks Sculpture Garden and Museum..
  46-47
Matthaei Conservatory and Nichols Arboretum 104
Memorial Falls, Munising...................................152
Michigan History Museum 40-41
Michigan Iron Industry Museum....................... 82-83
Michigan Science Center 16-17
Michigan Space Science Center 30
Michigan State Capitol................................... 42-43
Michilimackinac, Colonial................................ 62-63
mining...82-83, 90-91
Mio, bird watching near 132, 133
model ships, Dossin Great Lakes Museum...................27
Morley, Holt cemetery in....................................110
Munising
  Memorial Falls..152
  Pictured Rocks National Lakeshore 78-79
museums
  African American History............................. 14-15
  American Magic Museum 29
  art.. 98-99
  aviation 30-31

children's 112-113
Dossin Great Lakes Museum............................ 26-27
Great Lakes Shipwreck Museum....................... 72-73
Henry Ford Museum...................................... 22-23
Logging Museum 48-49
Marquette Maritime Museum 80-81
Marshall M. Fredericks Sculpture Garden and
Museum 46-47
Michigan History Museum 40-41
Michigan Iron Industry Museum 82-83
Museum of Ojibwa Culture 64-65
outdoor, see outdoor museums
music, Interlochen Center for the Arts 50-51

N
national forests
  Huron National Forest 132-133
  Sylvania Wilderness, Ottawa National Forest 86-87
national lakeshores
  Pictured Rocks 78-79
  Sleeping Bear Dunes.................................... 54-55
national park, Isle Royale 94-95
nature center, Kalamazoo................................. 32-33
Negaunee, Michigan Iron Industry Museum 82-83
Nelis' Dutch Village, Holland..................................34
Nichols Arboretum, Matthaei Conservatory and 104-105
Nip and Sip Drive-In restaurant, Lansing.................116
Norton Mound group (American Indian burial site) .110

O
Oden State Fish Hatchery................................. 56-57
Ojibwa Indians
  Museum of Ojibwa Culture 64-65
  Sleeping Bear Dunes National Lakeshore 54-55
Ojibwa Island Park, Saginaw..............................150
Old Growth Trail, Hartwick Pines State Park 48-49
Ontonagon, Porcupine Mountains Wilderness State Park
  88-89
Ottawa National Forest, Sylvania Wilderness......... 86-87
outdoor (campfire) cooking 107
outdoor museums
  Fort Wilkins Historic State Park 92-93
  Greenfield Village..................................... 20-21
  Keweenaw National Historic Park 90-91

P
Paradise
  Greta Lakes Shipwreck Museum........................ 72-73
  Tahquamenon Falls State Park........................ 70-71
  Whitefish Point Bird Observatory 68-69, 73
parks (See also gardens; state parks)
  Historic Mill Creek Discovery Park.................... 60-61
  Isle Royale National Park............................. 94-95
  urban.. 150-151
Petoskey Stones.................................... 100, 142-143
Petting Farm at Domino's Farms................... 122-123
Philip A. Hart Visitor Center 54
picnicking 146-147
  in urban parks 151
Pictured Rocks National Lakeshore..................... 78-79
pioneer cemeteries 110
planetarium, Michigan Science Center 16, 17
playdough, making..115
Point Betsie Lighthouse 138
Point Iroquois Light House 73

Polk Penguin Center..19
Porcupine Mountains Wilderness State Park.... 85, 88-89
Portage, Air Zoo at 30-31
pow wows 148-149
Presque Isle area, hiking in..88

Q

Quincy Mine Hoist, Mine, and Tram 90

R

reenactors, see living history
relaxation, value of..125
restaurants, drive-in 116-117
Richard and Jane Manoogian Ship Model Showcase....27
Rock Harbor..94
rock hunting.. 142-143
Rock of Ages Lighthouse 138

S

Saginaw
    Hoyt Main Library.. 136-137
    Marshall M. Fredericks Sculpture Garden 46-47
    urban parks in 150
sailing 52-53
sand dunes...54-55, 78-79
Sault Ste. Marie
    drive-in restaurant in 116
    shipping locks at.. 66-67
science center
    Michigan Science Center.................................... 16-17
    Michigan Space Science Center................................30
sculpture gardens/parks
    Frederik Meijers Gardens and Sculpture Park..... 36-37
    Marshall M. Fredericks Sculpture Garden and
    Museum 46-47
sea sickness, preventing..125
Seney National Wildlife Refuge 74-75
shipping/ships
    Dossin Great Lakes Museum............................... 26-27
    Locks at Sault Ste. Marie................................... 66-67
    Marquette Maritime Museum 80-81
    Tall Ship Sailing 52-53
shipwrecks 72-73, 139
Silver River Falls, Keweenaw Peninsula....................153
skiing (U.S. Hall of Fame)................................... 84-85
Sleeping Bear Dunes National Lakeshore.............. 54-55
snowboarding (U.S. Hall of Fame) 84-85
snowkiting.. 134, 135
Soo Locks 66-67
South Manitou Island Lighthouse............................138
Southfield, pioneer cemetery in 110
space exploration 30-31
St. Ignace, Museum of Ojibwa Culture................. 64-65
St. Joseph, children's museum in..............................112
St. Mary's River...66
Stannard Rock Lighthouse...138
State Capitol... 42-43
state parks
    Fayette Historic State Park................................. 76-77
    Fort Wilkins Historic State Park....................... 92-93
    Hartwick Pines State Park and Logging Museum48-49
    Porcupine Mountains Wilderness State Park 85, 88-89
    Tahquamenon Falls 70-71
Sturgeon River, waterfalls on 152
Subaru Noquemanon Ski Marathon, at Marquette......85

Summit Peak 88
sunburn, preventing...101
sunsets, viewing
    from beaches 78, 100
    from a canoe..87
Swedish cemetery, in Cheboygan 110
swimming..86
Sylvania Recreation Area..86
Sylvania Wilderness 86-87
    canoeing in...108

T

Tahquamenon Falls State Park 70-71, 152
train rides 96-97
Traverse City
    Manitou, tall ship in 52-53
    National Cherry festival in 144

U

Union Bay 88
Union Mine trail 88
United Presbyterian Church Cemetery, Southfield 110
urban parks 150-151
U.S. Forest Service.. 132, 133
U.S. Ski & Snowboard Hall of Fame.................... 84-85

V

SS Valley Camp (museum ship) 67
Veldheer Tulip Gardens, Holland................................34

W

waterfalls... 152-153
    Porcupine Mountains Wilderness State Park 88
    Tahquamenon Satte park...................................... 70-71
weather, experiencing and enjoying................... 140-141
    in winter.. 85, 154-155
Wellington Farm.. 122-123
Whitefish Point Bird Observatory 68-69, 73
Wickes Park, Saginaw..150
wilderness areas
    Porcupine Mountains Wilderness State Park 88-89
    Sylvania Wilderness.................................. 86-87, 108
Wildlife Interpretive Gallery, Detroit Zoo 18, 36
wildlife refuge 74-75
windchill..154
Windmill Island Gardens, Holland............................34
winter festivals/events 85, 154-155
woods/woodland
    forests. See national forests
    Hartwick Pines State Park and Logging Museum48-49
    Nichols Arboretum..104

Z

zoos, see Detroit Zoo

About the Authors

MIKE LINK

Mike Link is the author of 22 books and numerous magazine articles. He and his wife, Kate, live in Willow River, Minnesota where they enjoy having their grandchildren discover the world of nature and play. The bird feeders are always full and the forest has wonderful trails.

For 37 years Mike directed the Audubon Center and now entering retirement, he is looking forward to writing, teaching for both Northland College and Hamline University, and of course spending time with the grandchildren.

As his books attest, traveling is another passion. With fifty states and twenty countries covering his travels, paddles, hikes, and explorations, he feels that he owes a debt to the Earth. Whether we call it Mother Nature, Gaia, or Creation, the Earth is our source of air, water and sustenance and its destruction is a crime.

Son Jon, his wife, Kristin, and their daughter, Teagan, live in Bozeman, Montana, enjoying the mountains as often as possible. Daughter Julie lives in Champlin, MN with grandson Matthew. Mike's son Matt died in a kayak accident in New Zealand and little Matthew is a spirited tribute to his uncle. Daughter Alyssa, her husband, Troy and the three grandchildren (Ryan, Aren, Annalise) now live in Duluth, MN, which allows them to spend a lot more time together.

KATE CROWLEY

Since marrying Mike and moving to the country twenty-two years ago, she has been surrounded by forests, prairies, birds, dogs, cats, horses, and lots of other wild creatures. When Mike built her Lady Slipper Cottage in the woods, her dream expanded, but it wasn't complete until she became a grandmother.

Kate has been a naturalist, an educator, and a writer for 30 years, first at the Minnesota Zoo and the Audubon Center of the North Woods. She has co-authored 12 books with Mike, and writes for magazines and a monthly nature newspaper column. Kate enjoys hiking, biking, skiing, scrapbooking, reading and spending as much time as possible with her grandchildren. She cares deeply about preserving the natural world.